THE MEN IN MY LIFE

THE MEN IN MY LIFE

Vivian Gornick

A Boston Review Book

THE MIT PRESS Cambridge, Mass. London, England

MIT Press books may be purchased at special quantity
discounts for business or sales promotional use. For
information, please e-mail special_sales@mitpress.mit.edu or
write to Special Sales Department, The MIT Press,
55 Hayward Street, Cambridge, MA 02142.

This book was set in Adobe Garamond by *Boston Review*
and was printed and bound in the United States of America.

Library of Congress Cataloging-in-Publication Data
Gornick, Vivian.
  The men in my life / Vivian Gornick.
    p. cm.
  "A Boston Review book."
  ISBN 978-0-262-07303-5 (hardcover : alk. paper)
  1. American literature—History and criticism—Theory, etc.
2. English literature—History and criticism—Theory, etc.
3. Authorship—Psychological aspects. 4. Social problems in
literature. 5. Male authors—Appreciation. 6. Authorship—
Sex differences. 7. Literature and society. I. Massachusetts
Institute of Technology. II. Title.
  PS25.G67 2008
  810.9—dc22

                                        2008022927

10 9 8 7 6 5 4 3 2 1

CONTENTS

PREFACE

IN SCHOOL, THE TEACHER HELD A COMPO-
sition of mine up to the class when I was eight
years old and said, "This little girl is going to
be a writer." At home—where Marx, socialism, and the international working class were
articles of faith—my mother pressed my upper
arm between two fingers and said, "Never forget where you come from." Both events were
formative. I grew passionate over writing, and
the political-ness of life was never lost on me.
In my youth these twin influences made me
suffer. I thought them hopelessly oppositional,
and was tormented by the suspicion that ultimately I need choose one way of knowing

the world over the other. It was literature that spoke most thrillingly to what I was already beginning to call "the human condition," but when social injustice stared me in the face it was easy enough to trade in emotional nuance for doctrinaire simplicity. So one day it was exciting to say to myself, "The only reality is the system"; the next, I'd pick up *Anna Karenina*, and the sole reality of the system would do a slow dissolve.

I entered college, and somewhere in my junior year something interesting happened: a drama of internal anguish that subsumed all else began to unfold. The words "anxiety" and "depression" entered my vocabulary. Conflicts I had never before paid attention to became alarming. In no time at all an unimagined universe of interiority opened before me, one equipped with its own theory, laws, and language, and constituting a worldview that could account for: everything. This was strong stuff. Under its influence, both literature and politics began to lose their either/or power over me. I didn't stop reading, and I didn't stop signing petitions, but I no longer felt commanded to "choose."

Then, before I knew it, it was 1970, and feminism was standing boldly on the horizon, urging me to take in its wisdom. The unlived lives of women began to seem not simply a drama of the psyche, but a crime of historic intent that could be solved only through a movement for social justice. This was an insight that, to every generation of feminists since the Enlightenment, had come like Revelation; and, like Revelation, it lit up a convert's sky, coloring every feature of the human landscape. The kaleidoscope of life had been shaken and all the familiar pieces now formed a new design, one that illuminated the way we spoke, read, thought, and wrote. Keep looking through that prism, we told ourselves, and we'd have every explanation ever needed. Then, problematically, the design complicated itself once more.

Although the rhetoric continued to run high, soon enough '70s feminists came to realize that while they stood united in political analysis, ideology alone could not purge them of the pathological self-doubt that seemed every woman's bitter birthright. For that, another kind of struggle was required: one for which a man, not a woman, supplied the tag line. As Anton Chekhov so memorably put it, "Others made me a slave but I must squeeze the slave out of myself, drop by drop."

Suddenly, literature, politics, and analysis came together, and I began to think more inclusively about the emotional imprisonment of mind and spirit to which all human beings are heir. In the course of analytic time, it became apparent that—with or without the burden of social justice—the effort required to attain any semblance of inner freedom was extraordinary. Great literature, I then realized, is a record not of the achievement, but of the effort.

With this insight as my guiding light, I began to interpret the lives and work of women and men alike who had spent their years making literature. But it was in the lives of the men, especially, that one could see what it meant to wrestle with the demons. Here they were—talented, often brilliant, with infinitely more permission to do and be than women had ever known—and *they* were endlessly dragged about by conflicts they could neither give up nor bring under control. I could not but be moved—by the great and the humble alike—to pity and admiration for those who demonstrated repeatedly that to "be and do" is not a given.

V. S. Naipaul has, very nearly, been consumed by the raging self-hatred that powers his work; George Gissing labored under an equally strong self-loathing that made social exile his natural milieu. Randall Jarrell fed a passion for poetry on the fever of a defensive brashness that drove him, ultimately, into suicidal despair. While Loren Eiseley made anthropologic poetry out of an isolating depression of monumental proportions, Allen Ginsberg became a holy fool, and Dubus, Carver, and Ford licked their sentimentalized wounds in story after story. Then, of course, there are Saul Bellow and Phillip Roth, who have each produced brilliance upon brilliance out of an unremitting fury that he was born into a culture that persisted in telling him he had no *right* to measure up; theirs is a fiction that for forty years has screamed, "Don't tell *me* I don't run things around here!" Against—or because of, or in spite of, who knows?—such "disability," each and every one of these writers has converted neurotic necessity into literary virtue, and achieved work of lasting value that casts light on the time in which it was conceived.

If, indeed, criticism is autobiography, this book, then, is a collection of essays written in appreciation of the working lives of literary men by a woman whose critical faculties have been shaped by a passion for literature, a hard-won knowledge of inborn anxiety, and a compelled devotion to liberationist politics. It is this last, I think, that is most responsible for the perspective vital to the making of these essays. The re-awakening in my late youth of the centuries-long struggle for women's rights clarified the intimate relation between literature, emotional damage, and social history; made evident to me the organic nature of all that is meant by the word "culture." It is my great hope that the reader will experience the development of this perspective as I have: as an enrichment of the writing and reading experience.

THE MEN IN MY LIFE

George Gissing:
A Neurotic for Our Times

ONE OF THE GREAT NEUROTICS AMONG
nineteenth-century English urban novelists is
George Gissing, a writer whose damaged ego
forced him into an isolation of his own making from which, paradoxically, came books of
immense social intelligence, motivated by the
keenest of psychological insights. These insights
were the reward of a literary man whose private
torments had the great good luck to mesh with
a world of realities only too happy to mirror
his troubled soul. Gissing's twenty-two novels,
invariably set in the misery brought on by the
Victorian caste system—namely, the unhappi-

ness meted out to those born with brains and temperament, but neither money nor connection—are nearly all riddled through with the entrenched melancholy of a protagonist bent on nursing a lifelong sense of deprivation. No one could brood as profitably as he on the failings of a system that regularly drove men and women of merit into the emotional incapacity that ensures spiritual isolation. We know this character. He speaks to us. His angry, brilliant projections remind us of the intimate relation between neurosis and actuality, exactly as we might experience it.

Born in Exile is the most openly autobiographical of Gissing's novels. Here, he comes closest to acknowledging that "the system" alone cannot really be held responsible for the protagonist's defeated life. An impoverished man of thirty, intellectually superior, living alone in lodgings, boiling over with misanthropic unhappiness, Godwin Peak thinks he is a prickly misfit because society will not permit him to prosper. On the other hand, it is clearly because he *is* so prickly that he cannot gain the affection of those who might help him on his way. On vacation in Exeter, Godwin meets the conservative, well-to-do family of an old classmate. The father is a somewhat poetic man anxious to square religion with the new findings of science (this is the 1880s), and, attracted to these people (especially to the daughter), Godwin finds himself pretending to study for the ministry in order, he tells them, to achieve just such a rapprochement. He is, of course, lying—his friends know him as the most contemptuous of atheists—but, craving admission to this world, he feels justified in practicing the deception. When he is found out, he stands disgraced. He and the daughter had fallen in love, but now she refuses to marry him as it will mean cutting herself off from all she has ever known. Godwin goes abroad to regain his mental health, only to die conveniently in Vienna.

The strength of the novel lies in the sophisticated probing of self and world that goes on inside the protagonist. In his panic, Godwin obsesses over his predicament, alternately condemning and justifying his own behavior. But as his emotional reasoning comes clear, he sees that he has—always!—been driven to undo himself. At the very last, he confides to the high-minded woman he has won and lost:

> "My strongest emotions seem to be absorbed in revolt; for once that I feel tenderly, I have a hundred fierce, resentful, tempestuous moods. To be suave and smiling in common intercourse costs me an effort. I have to act the part, and this habit makes me skeptical, whenever I am really prompted to gentleness."

Now we've come to the heart of the matter. For Godwin Peak, the price of the world is internal exile: a circumstance that nourishes doubt and suspicion at a high level. If ever he is made welcome in genteel society, it is certain to be only because society doesn't know him for who and what he really is; it entertains a fantasy that is destined to be sabotaged: by our protagonist himself, if necessary.

It is this conviction of inescapable outsider-ness—stirred from within, fortified from with-out—that is Gissing's true territory. This is the inner condition he understands down to the bone. It is when he gets right inside the one who feels him or herself a born outsider that Gissing is remarkable. He is often thought of as something of a socialist or even a feminist, seeking redress for the grievances of caste, but he is in fact neither. He despised the working class (thought it composed of savages), de-plored women (inferior by nature), and loathed democracy (the rule of the mob). He cared only for what he thought of as society's time-hon-ored sacrifice of the exceptional spirit. Oppo-sition was his party standard. In this sense he bears favorable comparison with some of the great novelists of his time and place. Neither Hardy, James, nor Eliot had any more politics than did Gissing. They, too, were drawn to the spectacle of the individual spirit desolated by the lock-step coldness of respectable society.

GISSING WAS BORN IN 1857 IN YORKSHIRE, the son of a druggist who died young, consigning a wife and five children to genteel poverty. George, however, was a gifted student who won a scholarship to a college in Manchester, with the promise of another in the offing for London University. At school he did extraordinarily well, carrying off all the prizes and honors, and discovering that he was a born academic. Presumably, he was set for life. But already Gissing was beset by the fatal combination of pride and insecurity that, throughout his life, would encourage him to self-destruct. At eighteen, still a student at the college, he began to prowl the

8

streets in search of sexual adventure. Here he met and fell in love with a young prostitute named Nell Harrison. Gissing romanticized Nell, and her need of him, to a fare-thee-well. On the eve of graduation he was caught stealing money for her from a fellow student. Not only was he expelled from the college, he was sent to prison for a month. Like the French lieutenant's woman, he had married himself to shame. *Now* he was set for life.

After prison, the family packed him off to America for a year where he wandered aimlessly, wrote his first stories, and nearly perished of the loneliness that was to become his life's companion. Back in England, he went looking for Nell Harrison, found her and, astonishingly, married her. They came down to London, moved into "lodgings," and Gissing began both his struggle to write and his accommodation to the sense of stigma that had left him, in his own eyes, beyond the pale of respectable society. The marriage, of course, turned out pure hell, and within a few years the couple had separated.

This place—beyond the pale—was the one Gissing clearly needed to occupy, as he pursued it relentlessly throughout his short life (he died at forty-six). Not that actual circumstances didn't co-operate. Two English writers of disparate sensibility capture the situation neatly:

Gissing, George Orwell tells us, was indeed up against "the fog-bound, gas-lit London of the eighties, a city of drunken puritans, where clothes, architecture and furniture had reached their rock bottom of ugliness, and it was almost normal for a working-class family of ten persons to inhabit a single room." Here "[a] bookish, over-civilized man, in love with classical antiquity, found himself trapped in a cold, smoky, Protestant country where it was impossible to be comfortable without a thick padding of money between yourself and the outer world."

On the other hand, Virginia Woolf observes, by 1884 Gissing's books had begun to sell and he was making a living from them. Yet, he insisted on feeling as though "the Baker Street trains hissed their steam under his window, and the lodger downstairs blew his room out, and the landlady was insolent, and the grocer refused to send the sugar so that he had to fetch it himself, and the fog burnt his throat and he caught cold and never spoke to anybody for three weeks."

Literary people had begun to seek him out (H. G. Wells *insisted* on becoming a friend), but Gissing continued to experience himself as poor and alone, condemned to the company, if any, of the wretched of the earth. "It is my fate," he wrote to an acquaintance as late as 1890, "to be known by the first class people and to associate with the second class—even the third and fourth. It will always be so." It was a self-created loneliness that put him in the bind from which he could imagine no escape. To this same acquaintance he also wrote, "This solitude is killing me. I can't endure it any longer . . . I must resume my old search for some decent working-girl who will come and live with me. I am too poor to marry an equal, and cannot live alone." Sure enough, Nell Gissing died, alone in a London slum in 1888, and Gissing picked up a servant girl in the street who became his second wife and provided him with yet another disastrous marriage, this one ending in even worse degradation than had the first. Needless to say, the house was a war zone off-limits to anyone he might want to know.

The character who appears most often in Gissing's books is based on himself: the literary man of taste who has no money. Without money he cannot hope to marry well, or make a home to which he can invite friends. Thus, our protagonist is destined for solitariness and sexual starvation, both of which drive him into the complex circumstance that forms the plot of the novel wherein—whether the book is set among the London poor or among the London middle class—Gissing will make a thorough exploration of both the external and internal miasma into which poverty, obscurity, and mortified senses have plunged our man. *New Grub Street* is the book into which he poured every kind of outsider emotion attached to this character that he had ever known or imagined.

The scene is London's vast scribbling life in the 1880s. The characters are writers of all sorts—journalists, novelists, scholars, book reviewers, and hacks who act as "editors" to those intent on vanity press publication. The shared view is: if you write trash you succeed, if you write authentically you fail (God, do you fail!). There is not a writer alive who will not be startled, even frightened, by Gissing's life-like depiction of this scene: commercially blunt publishers, nasty editors running small-minded quarterlies, literature produced by the pound and paid for by the pound, the economic evil of the royalty and advance system, the soul-destroying insecurity of writers, both marginal and successful. No one has captured this life as fully, as lucidly, as madly as Gissing has here, in this extraordinary work.

The major characters are Edwin Reardon, a painfully high-minded author of serious novels (Gissing's stand-in), and Jasper Milvain, an up-and-coming literary journalist with a strong sense of the marketplace. Their women are a pair of cousins, Amy and Marian Yule. Amy is bright and shallow, Marian thoughtful and sensitive. Jasper and Amy will prevail, Edwin and Marian go under. Around these four is grouped a cast of minor characters distinguished for its range of meanness and nobility, and for the dazzle of its dialogue. Although the deck is stacked—sensibility will suffer, worldliness succeed—the delivery of narrative development through a wealth of conversation that is psychologically rich, intellectually probing, and invariably of an exhilarating length, makes the book a joy to read.

For this reader, however, Gissing's psychological brilliance comes most fully into focus when it applies itself not to starving writers or sensitive young men of no means, but to the women who, in the author's own time, began to proclaim themselves "new." Almost against his will (he really didn't like them), he took a close look and saw that it was through the "odd women" that he could most sympathetically—that is, most realistically—express the nature of the crippling self-divide experienced by those who know themselves to be categorically unwanted. These people embodied the double bind that he had spent his life obsessing over: that of the born outsider whose own inner turmoil helps call into radical question the subversive nature of organized social experience.

I FIRST CAME TO GISSING'S WORK TWENTY-five years ago when a friend urged on me *The Odd Women.* I re-read the book every six months for years. Great books about women in modern times had been written by men who were Gissing's contemporaries—within twenty years there had been Thomas Hardy's *Jude the Obscure,* Henry James's *Portrait of a Lady,* George Meredith's *Diana of the Cross-ways*—but, penetrating as these novels were, Gissing's was the one that spoke most directly to me. I could see and hear the characters as if they were women and men of my own acquaintance. I knew intimately what was tearing these people apart. What's more, I recognized myself as one of the "odd" women. Every fifty years from the time of the French Revolution, feminists had been described as "new" women, "free" women, "liberated" women—but Gissing had gotten it just right. We were the "odd" women.

The novel is set in London in 1887. Mary Barfoot, a gentlewoman in her fifties, is running a secretarial school to prepare middle-class girls for occupations other than that of teacher or governess. Her colleague is Rhoda Nunn, thirty years old, darkly handsome, highly intelligent, uncompromising in her open scorn for what she calls the slavery of love and marriage; there isn't an argument to be made in favor of legal union for which Rhoda doesn't have an instant comeback. Against these two are set a group of friends from Rhoda's girlhood: the three Madden sisters, daughters of a country doctor whose death has left them nearly penniless and fit for nothing, all their hopes pinned on a successful marriage for the youngest, pretty Monica. Enter Edmund Widdowson and Everard Barfoot—the first, a timid clerk in his forties, just come into a modest fortune, who picks Monica up on a Sunday afternoon in the park; the second, Mary's clever, well-to-do, strong-willed cousin whose intellectual sparring with Rhoda (the glory of the book) becomes steadily, and mutually, eroticized. The story of these four is the one that Gissing tracks with skill, patience, and immense understanding.

What, the book asks, are men and women to be, both for themselves, and for each other? One of the couples is un-schooled, un-intellectual, and socially humble, the other educated, ambitious, and further up on the scale of status; but in relation to this question all four are possessed of an innocence for which life makes no allowance. Monica will marry Widdowson, only to learn what a prison sentence marriage to a narrow, frightened man can be. Rhoda will fail to marry Barfoot, who challenges her to a free union that in the end she has neither the trust in him nor the confidence in herself to make. All will purchase experience at the expense of coming a cropper.

To Edmund Widdowson (hungry to escape his shabby loneliness), marriage is the promise of a morally uplifting contract between a benign master and an obedient subordinate; he cannot imagine a partnership of equals. To Monica Madden, desperate to come in out of the economic cold, it is a calculated hope that some measure of comfort and security will be decently achieved. Soon enough, Widdowson is mortified by Monica's minimal assertions of independence, and grows despotic; she, in turn, is horrified at finding herself a bird in a gilded cage, and begins to despair. Their situation is pathos itself: "She asked only to be trusted and this, in spite of all, was beyond his power. In no woman on earth could he have put perfect confidence. He regarded them as born to perpetual pupilage . . . incapable of attaining maturity . . . imperfect beings ever liable to be misled."

Rhoda Nunn and Everard Barfoot, ambitious to occupy a world of "new" women and men, imagine themselves dedicated to the proposition of true partnership between the sexes, but in the final analysis can do no better than Monica and Widdowson. Theirs is the two steps forward, one step back journey into self-knowledge that accounts for the snail's pace at which internal change—social or emotional—progresses.

Barfoot's intelligence persuades him that he seeks companionate-ness in marriage. "For him [it] must mean . . . the mutual incitement of vigorous minds. Passion—yes, there must be passion at all events to begin with. [But] be a woman what else she may, let her have brains and the power of using them . . . intellect was his first requirement." At the same time, an appetite for mastery exerts as strong, if not stronger, a pull on him. Side by side with the pleasure Rhoda's intelligence gives him, his thoughts yet linger on how much "a contest between his will and hers would be an amusement decidedly to his taste . . . It would delight him to enrage Rhoda and then to detain her by strength, to overcome her senses, to watch her long lashes droop over the eloquent eyes . . ."

As for Rhoda—absolute in her conviction that women first and foremost must become "rational and responsible human beings"—she pronounces regularly on her position with a defensive bluntness that betrays her own emo-

20

tional ignorance. When Barfoot chides her proud severity—"Perhaps you make too little allowance for human weakness"—she replies coldly, "Human weakness is a plea that has been much abused, and generally in an interested spirit." Everard thrills to this response, but it also makes him smile. The smile frightens Rhoda into rudeness: "Mr. Barfoot, I have had enough of this . . . If you are practicing your powers of irony, I had rather you chose some other person. I will go my way, if you please."

In truth, the exchange excites them both. The attraction between them is rooted in the classical antagonism of sexual infatuation at its most compelling and its most exhausting. Bereft of tenderness or sympathy, it both draws and repels; wears away at the nerves; consumes itself in self-division and self-regard. A year and many remarkable conversations later, when his feeling for Rhoda is considerably advanced, Barfoot is yet of two minds: "Loving her as

21

he had never thought to love, there still remained with him so much of the temper in
which he first wooed her that he could be satisfied with nothing short of unconditional surrender." Concomitantly, Rhoda—her senses
fully aroused for the first time in her life—is
rapidly losing the comfort of her brash cer-
tainties. Now, openly drawn to Everard, she is
gripped by anxiety at the thought of yielding
to desire; insecurity and trepidation become
her daily companions.

Ultimately, however many words are spilled
among all four, the men are undone by the need
to master, and the women by the power of self-
doubt. Monica and Widdowson come literally
to disaster, Barfoot retreats into a conventional
marriage, and Rhoda achieves a sexless independence. For one brief moment only, a small
part of each of these people had reached out to
embrace the difficulty of struggling toward the
integrity required to form a "new" alliance—
and had then fallen back to that place in the

spirit where it is acceptable to no longer go on making the effort. The intelligence and writing skill exerted in tracing this entire experience place Gissing squarely in the company of the modernist masters of realist fiction.

For me, it has always been especially absorbing to follow Rhoda Nunn as both her polemics and her emotions flare, and we see that she cannot manage the consequences that the conflict between the two have set in motion. It is her confusion that makes her so real. Hardy's Sue Bridehead, James's Isabel Archer, Meredith's Diana are all magnificent creatures—and all similarly confused, if you will—but it is in Rhoda that I see myself, and others of my generation, *plain*. No other writer has captured the progress of our smarts, our anxieties, our bravado as *exactly* as has Gissing by putting Rhoda Nunn through some very recognizable paces. Imagine (as I can all too readily), the joy of that cold passion with which she, having seen the feminist light, pronounces, no equality in love? I'll do without! Children and motherhood? Unnecesssary! Social castigation? Nonsense! Between the ardor of Rhoda's rhetoric and the dictates of flesh-and-blood reality lies a no-man's-land of untested conviction. How easy it was—for us as well as Rhoda—to call out angrily, "To hell with all that!" How chastening to experience the uncontrollable force of feeling that steadily undermines these defiant simplicities. As Rhoda moves inexorably toward the moment when she fails herself, she becomes a walking embodiment of the gap between theory and practice: the place in which so many of us have found ourselves, time and again.

Although she and Barfoot are intellectually agreed that formal marriage is degrading to the spirit, when he suggests that they live together in a union free of legal connection, Rhoda, to her own great surprise, shrinks from the potential fallout of such a move. She finds that she dreads being reduced by the feelings of jealousy and abandonment that are certain to overwhelm her, should Barfoot ever betray her. She then realizes that she trusts him no more than Widdowson trusts Monica. In reality, it is herself she does not trust, herself she cannot depend on, herself at whose hands she fears betrayal, but this she does not yet understand. She only knows that to live as Barfoot suggests they live is to risk ending up a humiliated woman with the door of social acceptance closed in her face.

Barfoot, enjoying himself hugely, pushes her to the wall. It is agreed that "a day's walk among the mountains" will, once and for all, clarify their situation. And indeed, like the walk taken by Lily Bart and Laurence Selden in *The House of Mirth,* it proves decisive. As the path takes Rhoda and Barfoot higher and higher up the mountain, their familiar pleasure in one another's company flourishes: hope and desire renew themselves. But the longer they walk—talking, of course, all the way—the more complicated their feelings grow. Inevitably, each one expresses a sentiment or a point of view that the other finds off-putting. Descending the mountain, doubt and self-protectiveness steadily replace warmth and the willingness to trust; a sense of insult and injury pervades the atmosphere. The day ends with them plighting their troth, but within twenty-four hours the compact falls to pieces. They part with half-hearted assurances that they may yet repair, but we know their separation is a foregone conclusion.

For Barfoot, the promise and the failure of their adventure is something of an entertainment; it is with more relief than regret that he retreats to the place where he is certain to regain his social footing. For Rhoda, the episode is a misadventure that trips her up badly; in fact, it is life-changing. It has come home forcibly to her that her dream of men and women coming together in equal partnership, should they only be intellectually informed, is utopian. She sees how easily the vision is brought down by the disruptive claims of one's own conflicted self. It is fortification from the inside out that is wanted—the kind accomplished only by those prepared to do battle for a piece of emotional ground that must be taken again and again before it is actually secured.

Rhoda Nunn is, I believe, the protagonist in whom Gissing saw himself more clearly than in any other of his fictional creations; certainly she is the one given the least melodramatic of destinies. At the end of the novel, she is left neither defeated nor triumphant—rather, she is sobered. She has forfeited the invigorating innocence that kept her such exciting company, but her hard-won loneliness is an initiation. She sees the world and herself in it more clearly than she had before. She stands at the beginning of experience. That Gissing brings his odd woman to rest at this juncture is his great achievement.

H.G. Wells:
The Beginning of Wisdom

I'VE BEEN REREADING H. G. WELLS'S
Experiment in Autobiography once a year now
for the past few years. When I'm asked, "Why?"
(which is often) I'm tempted to answer by quot-
ing my mother. When she was in her eighties,
and living alone, I once gave her a copy of the
memoir of an Englishwoman, older than herself, who had written many novels and lived a
life as different from hers as any two lives could
be. A week later I found her reading the book
as though in a trance. "How are you liking
it?" I asked. She looked up at me, remained
silent for a moment, and then said, "I feel as

though she's in the room with me." And then she said, "When I finish this book I'm going to be lonely."

My feeling exactly about Wells's *Experiment*.

H. G. Wells sat down in 1932, at the age of sixty-five, to write his autobiography in order, he said, that he might find the peace necessary to go on trying to write the major book that would make up for all the less than major ones—then close to sixty volumes of novels, stories, and nonfiction—that he had already written. At this late date he still felt that he had not fully served his lifelong passion: scientific socialism and the hope of a world state. The thought of outliving this devotion without having achieved ultimate clarity on it haunted him. "The conception of a worker concentrated on the perfection and completion of a work," he said, was "a primary idea. Either the toad which is struggling to express itself here, *has* engendered a jewel in its head or it is nothing

worth troubling about in the way of toads . . .
This work [is the] jewel in my head for which
I take myself seriously enough to be self-scru-
tinizing."

Like many other writers of his time, Wells
thought of himself as a Man of the Future but
his style of self-presentation remained Victorian. His, he insisted, was a life no different
in its beginnings or its potential from that of
millions of others. He wished only, he said
repeatedly, to put his "personal origins into
the frame of human history and show how
the education that shaped [him] . . . was related to the great change in human conditions"
that had been gathering force for three cen-
turies "to disperse the aristocratic estate system . . . promote industrial co-ordination . . .
necessitate new and better informed classes
. . . break down political boundaries everywhere
and bring all men into one planetary community." To see his own life in this light—as the
exemplar of an ordinary, representative brain

alive at a telling moment in social history—was to understand the times in which he and his readers were living.

Yet, within a few paragraphs of this statement, Wells also tells us that he has never entirely loved any one person, place, or thing. It was not in him, he observes. Now that he is looking more closely at himself, he perceives something odd in his own make-up. "I am," he confesses, "rarely *vivid* to myself." That is, "never wholly or continuously interested, prone to be indolent and cold-hearted. I am readily bored." When he tries to make up for what he takes to be a character flaw, he inevitably finds himself acting a part. He becomes falsely charming and feels as though he is hiding out inside. "You will," he forewarns the reader, "discover a great deal of evasion and refusal in my story."

I take all this to mean that Wells unknowingly suffered from low-grade depression most of his life. Now, there is nothing more interesting or rewarding in a memoir than the narrative of a life made dramatic by conscious worldliness in struggle with unconscious melancholia. In the case of such superior examples as De Quincy's *Confessions of an English Opium Eater* or Loren Eiseley's *All The Strange Hours,* the result is stirring. In the case of *Experiment in Autobiography* the result, for this reader at least, is more moving than can perhaps be said.

HERBERT GEORGE WELLS WAS BORN IN 1866 in a small town in England, the third son of a gardener and a lady's maid who, upon marriage, bought a crockery shop that did not succeed and did not quite fail. Consequently, the entire family lived for more than two decades in a dank basement apartment below the shop, the memory of which made Wells shudder well into middle age. When Bertie (as he was called) was fourteen years old, he, like his brothers before him, and like nearly every boy in the British lower and lower middle classes of the time, was apprenticed, in his case to a draper: "'put to trade' and bound, before we could exercise any choice in the matter." Unlike his brothers, however, Bertie rebelled—"I would not, I could not give myself satisfactorily to this strange restricted life"—and the draper let him go. His parents were appalled. One wretched attempt to apprentice him followed another, and finally he battled his way to school where, of course, he instantly shone.

In no time at all, Wells got himself a provincial education, developed a love of science, made his way to London, became a student and then a teacher at the Normal School for Science, married a cousin who'd been his childhood friend, discovered that sexual unhappiness was unbearable to him, ran off with one of his students (who became the second Mrs. Wells), was moved to write a tale of scientific fantasy (*The Time Machine*), and the rest was history. In fairly short order he rose to become H. G. Wells, the rich and famous author of innumerable tales and works of nonfiction influenced by the utopian prospect of a future world community wherein internal freedom would blossom and thrive in each and every human being. Soon, he was living one of the most sophisticated lives in Europe. He traveled constantly, occupied residences both in London and the country, knew everyone worth knowing, was both guest of and host to the great and the near great: artists, industrialists, heads of state; delighting as well in exotics, eccentrics, and thirty-minute wonders. He enjoyed it all, and he had it all.

It is impossible to over-emphasize what loving the physical sciences did for Wells. Like any true writer, he instantly turned his passion into a metaphor. "I did not at first link the idea of science with the socialist idea, the idea, that is, of a planned inter-coordinated society," but very soon he saw that a synthesis of the sciences led to a visionary interpretation of a new world, one in which, after socialism came, "life would be valiant and spacious and there would be no more shabbiness or darkness in the world."

This vision required another element necessary for human fulfillment—that of sexual liberation: pleasure freely sought and freely taken. ("To the dismay of the Fabians and the immense embarrassment of Labour Party socialists, I began to sexualize socialism.") As a teenager Wells had resented, even more than being forced into the apprenticeship, the proscription against sexual gratification. The puritanism of Victorian society seemed even more cruel to him than being "jammed for life into laborious, tedious, uninteresting, and hopeless employments," and before he had come of age, his thinking on the subject had helped give him the broad outlines of the ideas that would dominate his adult life.

In practice this meant that Wells, espousing the doctrine of Free Love, pursued women steadily and relentlessly for the whole of his adult life; the intensity of sexual renewal was his necessity, and he thought neither he nor anyone else should do without. Convinced that he was serving a principled article of faith, he conducted his many affairs with the knowledge and apparent consent of the sexually faint-hearted wife whom he had persuaded that his sleeping with other women need not disturb their firmly anchored family life. In fact, Wells kept Jane Wells apprised of his every amorous adventure; she, in turn, often sent gifts and invitations to the mistress of the moment.

In treating of this distinctly odd turn of events, Wells insists:

> I was following a road along which at variable paces a large section of the intelligentsia of my generation was moving in England, towards religious skepticism, socialism, and sexual rationalism . . . Ultimately, I was to come to a vision of a possible state of affairs in which scarcely one familiar landmark would remain.

This passage says much about how Wells the writer and ideologue helped Wells the man describe himself to himself; it also sheds light on the virtues and shortcomings of certain of his imaginative works. Although Wells wrote many tales of science fiction fantasy along with his many books of serious nonfiction on history, politics, and economics, he also wrote realistic novels. In the novels, not a single character has an inner life independent of a position, an attitude, a social point of view. In the celebrated quarrel between Wells and Henry James over the art of the novel, James held to the conviction that the characters were the story, and the world the frame around them, while Wells said, "Nonsense. We are living in a world that intrudes itself everywhere: the frame is getting into the picture." The outcome: James made art, Wells made polemics. The best thing in his novels is the naked delight that Wells—and thus the reader—takes in the lucid style of description-informed-by-analysis that he developed as an intellectually gifted journalist best equipped for social criticism.

Yet somewhere inside himself, Wells knew that the emotional reality beneath the social problematic is complex, not simple, and *experiment* is most illuminating when (for a moment here and there) he makes himself see and feel the cost of his "principled experimentation" with open marriage. Wells's "compromise" with his wife began five years after their marriage in 1895, when she proved to be companionate but no longer sexually responsive. Even as he is rehearsing this history in his most "let's be reasonable about this" tone of voice, this is how he reflects on the actuality of the situation:

> The modus vivendi we contrived was sound enough to hold us together to the end, but it was by no means a perfect arrangement . . . it was an experiment in adjustment but there was nothing exemplary about it . . . We [both] supposed there were restless spirits with a craving for variety. What could be more rational than

39

for such super-animated men and women to find out and assuage one another?

And everything else would remain as it was before.

But as a matter of fact, short of some rare miracle of flatness, nothing does remain as it was before. Two worlds are altered every time a man and woman associate.

Three or four, actually, if the association includes adultery.

Wells continued writing his autobiography long after *Experiment* was published in 1934. These additions—which he called *Postscript to Experiment*—were published in 1984, forty years after his death in 1946, in a single volume edited by his son and entitled *H. G. Wells in Love*. The book is a full account of the love life he did not feel free to discuss in print during his own lifetime, and it is remarkable for what it reveals, both wittingly and unwittingly—especially unwittingly.

The opening section consists of an introduction Wells wrote to a publication called *The Book of Catherine Wells,* a gathering of stories and literary fragments that Jane Wells left behind when she died in 1927. The title alone is thought provoking, as during her marriage to Wells she was known only as Jane, never as Catherine. Wells explains that soon after their marriage he proposed to his wife (whose birth name was Amy Catherine) that "for everyday use and our common purposes" he rename her Jane, and she agreed. Without batting an eye, Wells had written in *Experiment*:

> Catherine Wells was indeed not quite one of us, not quite one with Jane and me, I mean; she was a quiet, fine spirited stranger in our household . . . Our union had never incorporated her. I had glimpses of her at times; she would look at me out of Jane's brown eyes and vanish.

Now in *Postscript* he continues:

Jane was a person of much greater practical ability than Catherine . . . She ordered a house well and was an able 'shopper,' she helped people in difficulties and stood no nonsense from the plumber. Her medicine cupboard at home was prepared for all occasions. She had gone through a Red Cross course so as to be competent in domestic emergencies. She had a file of shop addresses where things needed could be bought. Her garden was a continually glowing success.

She also typed Wells's manuscripts, paid his bills, listened to him talk his way into his next book, accompanied him on formal occasions and, above all, made it impossible for him to marry any one of his many mistresses, as he always made it abundantly clear that under no circumstances would he divorce Jane. Eventually, it was Catherine, not Jane, who took rooms of her own in Bloomsbury where she went on occasion to write and be alone with herself: rooms that H.G. never laid eyes on.

It is painful to realize that he seems never to have reflected on the meaning of his having pushed another human being out of shape entirely for the sake of his own comfort. He, who had spilled a river of words in defiance of the mental and emotional straitjacket that Victorian marriage so often became, did not ever consider that he had condemned the expressive life of his nearest and dearest relative to internal exile.

On the other hand, Wells puts it all down for *us* to see what he himself cannot see. He wanted the two books of autobiography to be published together, as he rightly felt that it was only as a whole that his life could be accurately reviewed. Taken as an attempt—sometimes genuine, sometimes not—to understand his own sexual drives, and the part they played in his inner development, it is impossible not to experience *H. G. Wells in Love* as a remarkable document in the history of literary self-examination.

Beginning with an open admission of secretly proud male randiness—"Even now I smirk if anyone suggests that I have been a gay lad in these matters"—Wells moves seamlessly to another admission: his lifelong fantasy of an ideal of romantic love he calls the Lover-Shadow. He never perceives that these are two sides of the same coin, but he does see the instrumental nature of most of the adventuring he has done with women for whom he too was only a means to an end: "I was loved as I loved," he says flatly. "[T]he exchanges were fairly equal—two libertines met—and when I *got* a woman, a woman *got* a man."

Along the way, there were a number of major affairs. Amber Reeves: "She aroused a storm of sexual obsession in me"; Rebecca West: "We loved each other in bright flashes; we were mutually abusive; we were fundamentally incompatible"; Odette Keun: "A thoroughly nasty and detestable person; vain, noisy and weakly outrageous . . . She excited me a great deal";

Moura Budberg, more important than all the others put together. It was through his feeling for her—feeling that would not die even when his vanity was wounded by it—that Wells, in his final years, was forced into the prolonged reflection on romantic love that truly deepened his understanding of self-and-world, and made of him the sympathetic figure whose company this reader has a yen for at least once a year.

Wells met Moura Budberg in Russia in 1920 when he was interviewing Maxim Gorky and she, a woman of twenty-seven, was the writer's secretary. They had a brief but intense encounter at that time, and did not meet again for some ten years, by which time Jane Wells was dead. When Moura—by all accounts a woman of great appeal—moved to London, she became a figure in Russian émigré society as well as in the many circles that Wells frequented. They both fell seriously in love, and soon enough he proposed that they marry. She turned him down. It suited her to go on as they were, joined in an intimacy that allowed each of them the freedom to be themselves. She prized her independence, her separate world of Russian émigrés, her need to come and go without accountability.

Wells was shocked—he could hardly believe that Moura did not wish to merge her life with his—to become, as he put it, "a world-interested woman to my world-interested man"—and he felt bitter toward her. Then, when he discovered that she often lied to him—it has been established that Moura Budberg did some spying for the Soviets—and he was forced to understand that she *really* had a life to which he was not privy, he was stunned; stunned and outraged, even frightened, but above all, jealous—not of other men, but of her life apart. Yet he could not separate from her. She delighted and compelled him. She was, he said, a creature of impulse who had moments of extraordinary wisdom that could "illuminate a question suddenly like a burst of sunshine on a wet February day." He adored sleeping with her. Then, as ever, he could not do without.

They quarreled and parted repeatedly, and repeatedly they came together again. The most interesting and admirable pages in the *Postscript* are those wherein Wells grapples daily, sometimes hourly, with the difficulty of understanding this relationship that brings neither peace nor fulfillment, yet remains magnetizing. When he takes in the fact that she is "fundamentally indifferent to my dream" and still he cannot break with her, that is the beginning of wisdom for him. It is then that he starts to ponder the reality of being attached to a person who is as complicated as he, one whose inner needs are as articulated as his own, and are *different* from his own. It precludes the fantasy of "two shall be as one," and forces on him the realization that Moura is first and foremost not a woman, but a separate being. The information transmutes into knowledge that is not unwelcome, but it saps the connection of exhilaration. There was no longer any question of not staying together, "But we were no longer the happy and confident lovers we had been."

Time passes. He drifts, has brief affairs, travels alone. "I doubt if we shall ever have quite done with each other," he winds up.

There is an irrational gravitation between us . . . We seem destined to remain in this state of loose association, like double stars that rotate about each other but never coalesce. Our very looseness now averts a conclusive rupture . . . It is absurd to say I am still in love. And yet I love . . . I doubt if we love each other very much, continuously and steadily . . . Our affection, our pity for each other, may have deepened, our helpfulness maybe, and our mutual toleration. But to get to know each other [as] intimately as we have, has been to lay bare our immense incompatibilities and console rather than compensate each other for them.

This was written in the summer of 1935. In November of that same year Wells wrote,

> The fact remains that when all is said and done, she is the woman I really love. I love her voice, her presence, her strength and her weaknesses. I am glad whenever she comes to me. She is the thing I like best in life . . . my nearest intimate . . . the dearest thing in my affections. And so she will remain to the end.

Which she did.

When I first read *Experiment in Autobiography*, I loved Wells for the extraordinary directness of his voice (I felt him as a friend speaking openly and without reserve right at me), and I envied him, that he could have lived almost an entire life within the embrace of an unaltered belief in the coming of the world state, while I have had to wander in the wilderness of seeing all such hopes repeatedly smashed underfoot. But as I have reread the book over the years I have come to cherish him not only because he had grown wise, but because until the very end of his life he was still trying to make sense of things.

It was the jealousy that had done it. He hadn't counted on that. The irrationality of it; the disruptive power of the suffering it caused. Now, he was something like the doctor in Chekhov's novella *Ward Six,* the one who couldn't understand what it meant to be bodily confined until he himself was so confined. Had Jane suffered jealousy? Or any of the other women he'd made care for him, and then been flagrantly unfaithful to? Whenever one had complained or made a scene, he'd simply considered her an irrational hysteric. Now, however, he began to see that scientific socialism would not be as easy to achieve as he had originally thought. There were all these intangibles in the human make-up, the drives that reason could not influence, the ones that would always subvert rational needs in a rational society.

It is the silent, wondering *feel* of this kind of speculativeness, running just beneath the surface of the prose, that makes me cherish Wells more each time I read his *Experiment*. To find oneself in the presence of an articulated human being who, in his sixties and seventies, is alive to the ongoing task of thinking hard about his experience—nothing gets consigned to the written-off past—what a gift! The depth of such reflectiveness is precious. It tells of a man struggling not only to understand how he came to be, but to puzzle out where he is now, *right now,* in the ever-accumulating now. Ultimately, this is what makes him a trustworthy narrator: we feel him alone with himself in the presence of the reader. More one cannot ask of a memoirist.

Wells's final years were spent in a richly sustaining loneliness. He was alive in his head more completely than ever before. He had the recognition of Moura Budberg's full humanity not only to keep him company, but to guide his thought still further.

Loren Eiseley:
Excavating the Self

LOREN EISELEY—ANTHROPOLOGIST AND
poet—spent forty years looking at bones, animals, and oceans with an instinctive sense
of metaphor applied to all his findings. His
writings—essays and poems that blend the
scientific and the literary—are memorable for
the singular detachment they bring to large,
poetic evocations of geologic time, unearthed
civilizations, the evolutionary nature of all
that lives. In his essays Eiseley is a voyager
steering a narrow course that widens steadily
into a largeness of consideration that is by
no means sanguine: everywhere there is loss,
threat, confusion.

For Eiseley the universe is not filled with loneliness, the universe *is* loneliness. The condition is elemental: into it we are born, out of it we fashion ourselves. Afflicted with an abiding loneliness of his own, Eiseley chose to observe isolation in the universe on a grand scale, and made of it his lasting subject. In time, the preoccupation with humanity and its surround aroused philosophic questions not of survival but of being. The isolation posed as much promise as threat. Self-creation, he speculated, is the privilege, not the obligation, of the race. What Eiseley himself was able, and not able, to do with such knowledge is the subject of this essay.

The gaze of the man behind the unsparing observation of what we are and where we come from is calm, open, unagitated, resolved upon the integration of whatever comes into view. So successful is the merger between narrator and subject in these essays contemplating a world with or without dinosaurs, or flowers, or starfish, that the reader might justifiably conclude the writer is himself a man long emerged from his own chaos, now working in a state of planetary equilibrium.

The tone of the essays is the tone Eiseley meant to apply to the memoir that he completed shortly before his death in 1977. He intended that this book—*All The Strange Hours*—would present its protagonist not intimately, but within a scope of consideration equal to the one he had applied all his working life as an anthropologist. He would treat himself much as he would any other specimen he might be digging out. In fact, the memoir is subtitled "an excavation." Early family life would be sketched only broadly; sex, marriage, and friendship spoken of not at all; neither would we learn much about the author as a figure in the world. We were to view him as kind of prototypic being alive on the planet at this time, in this place. The book he actually wrote is remarkable because the writing welled up out of a place beyond the reach of conscious intent, and it rescued its author repeatedly from his own defensiveness, taking the work ever more inward until the memoir did that astonishing and mysterious thing that good writing does: became something larger than the sum of its parts, achieved an inner life that can truly be called haunting.

LOREN EISELEY WAS BORN IN 1907 IN Nebraska. His father was a decent man who read books and seemed to fail at almost everything he tried. His mother was stone-deaf and had once been beautiful; deafness and anger led her to become a creature of gutteral sound, wary and at bay. Her presence all day long was lonely-making. The father loved him, but his love did not reduce the loneliness. Within himself, the boy turned away to the glorious emptiness before him, to the birds and animals, the fossils and desert striations to be found out on the sun-baked Nebraska plain. Here, in *this* silence, he did not feel alone.

The father died; there was no money; the boy dropped out of school, left home at nineteen, and began to wander. "All over America men were drifting like Sargasso weed in a vast dead sea of ruined industry," among them the young Loren Eiseley. The Depression suited him fine. Riding the rails, surviving in hobo encampments, enduring the brutishness of a world hung with the sign "Jobless men keep going," confirmed him (even then) in his belief that "There is nothing more alone in the universe than man . . . Only . . . rarely and in hidden moments of communion with nature, does man briefly escape his solitary destiny."

In his late twenties Eiseley broke out of the long cycle of poverty and wandering, returned to school, became an anthropologist with a strong talent for writing, went on to graduate school, and a life in teaching and university administration. He wrote many books of essays and poetry, all meant to "excavate" the relationship between man and the animals, man and

57

the elements, man and the universe, man and anything but other people. Throughout his life Eiseley experienced himself as a solitary. It matters not that he was, in fact, married and had friends, colleagues, and students in abundance; it matters only that this is how he saw himself. A man alone among men became the organizing principle of his inner life. As the years went on, and the books piled up, he became persuaded that he had always been destined for the company of the universe, not of human fellowship—and that, he told himself, was fine, just fine. When Eiseley sat down to write his memoir he considered himself both knowing, and at peace, on that score. Yet the prose, almost from the start, strikes an acutely emotional note distinctly at odds with that measured consideration.

Not more than twenty pages in, Eiseley casually describes his mother as "paranoid, neurotic and unstable"—terms of description unalarming to the reader of modern memoir—but then, in an unexpected outburst, he also writes:

> There will be those to say in this mother-worshipping culture that I am harsh, embittered. They will be quite wrong. Why should I be embittered? It is far too late. A month ago, after a passage of many years, I stood above her grave in a place called Wyuka. We, she and I, were close to being one now, lying like the skeletons of last year's leaves in a fence corner. And it was all nothing. Nothing, do you understand? All the pain, all the anguish. Nothing. We were, both of us, merely the debris life always leaves in its passing, like the maimed discarded chicks in a hatchery tray—no more than that. For a little longer I would see and hear, but it was nothing, and to the world it would mean nothing.

The passage is startling The directness jars. The directness and the nakedness. It's the "Nothing, do you understand?" that does it. In that quivering insistence we feel the presence of a sixty-seven-year-old man whose thin skin is still stretched across an open wound.

A few pages later Eiseley describes a dinner with W. H. Auden, who was a great admirer of his work. The dinner goes badly. By his own admission, he'd been feeling uncomfortable with the great poet, diminished somehow in his presence. Auden, aware of the stiffness between them, is chatting to set them at ease. He asks Eiseley (the men are the same age) what the first public event is that he remembers, and offers, briefly, that for himself it was the sinking of the Titanic in 1912. Eiseley replies by falling into an extended reverie over a prison break that took place near his home (also in 1912), letting his voice go self-consciously "poetic" as he speaks ("He blew the gates with nitroglycerin. I was five years old . . . already old enough to know one should flee from the universe but I did not know where to run . . . There was an armed posse and a death . . . We never made it."). The tale is long, self-dramatizing, and unmistakably competitive. Yet we are touched, not embarrassed, by it because we've already been given a taste of the rawness inside the man.

To a considerable degree, the entire memoir is an ever deepening clarification of these two passages. Chapter headings may read "The Rat that Danced" or "Toads and Men" or "The Coming Of the Giant Wasps," but we are engaged by the man who told us more than he meant to tell himself when he rapped out, "Nothing, do you understand?" and then, almost immediately, related the story of his dinner with Auden. What *that* man is grappling with is the experience this reminiscence wants to shape.

It is in the chapters on the wandering years that we first meet the man who identifies with animals, not with people: feel the weight and consequence of his grievance. In some of the best Depression writing you will ever read, Eiseley evokes the despairing antagonism of the time: a kind of starved, murderous haze that keeps drifting up from the middle of the socialized world. Tramping through some terrible little town in the California desert where the vagrant is the enemy ("Jobless men keep going"), he thinks:

> If you turn backward you will find only shutters banging in the wind, smashed windowpanes, the eyes of strangers, or, worse, the eyes of those who know you so thoroughly they wish never to see you again . . . The rules were very simple in that place . . . the citizen didn't count. All that mattered were the watchers who ate and slept, and the watched who were unsuccessful at either.

Once, during this period, a vicious brakeman tried to push him off a moving train. "He struck me across the face and pushed," Eiseley writes. "A thin hot wire like that in an incandescent lamp began to flicker in my brain . . . 'Kill him, kill him,' blazed the red wire. 'He's trying to kill you.'" Hours later, in a hobo camp, he is asked about his swollen face. When he explains, the man who questioned him (as though taking his cue from Steinbeck) says, "Just get this straight . . . The capitalists beat men into line. Okay? The communists beat men into line. Right again? . . . Men beat men, that's all. That's all there is. Remember it, kid." Of this exchange Eiseley remarks with some irony: "That man whose name I never knew . . . left all my life henceforward free of mobs and movements, free as only very wild things are both solitary and free." But the real conclusion of the story comes when Eiseley observes of himself that often, over the years, in trying to tell what he knows, he has felt that "the tale I had intended . . . had been lost in the incoherence of a split personality, the murderer who had not murdered but who carried a red wire glowing in his brain."

Of this man—the civilized writer with the red wire still glowing in his brain—he speaks rarely and only indirectly. The indirection leads him into dark waters:

> Men should discover their past. I admit to this. It has been my profession. Only so can we learn our limitations and come in time to suffer life with compassion. Nevertheless, I now believe there are occasions when . . . to tamper with the past, even one's own, is to bring [on] that slipping, sliding horror which revolves around all that is done, unalterable, and yet which abides unseen in the living mind . . . [and makes] us lonely beyond belief.

Ostensibly, he is speaking here of the unexpected consequences of one or two world-famous excavations, but of course that is not what he is speaking of at all. This far I go, the writing says, and no farther.

So the memoir proceeds, from subject to subject—his own early digs, the writing of his books, the years as a university teacher and administrator, archaeologists he has admired—relentlessly seeking detachment and poetic sentence-making, but repeatedly giving way to the pull of a melancholy too compelling for the memoirist to ignore, too congealed for him to unpack.

In a memorable chapter called "Madeline," we are told of a cat Eiseley lived with in graduate school who, desperate for recognition, discovered a talent that made his room-mates cheer: she could bow. The more the students cheered, the more Maddy bowed. Soon she was bowing as though for her very life and they were all, especially Eiseley, trapped by the cat's need for their applause:

> She lived for it; one could not let her down, humiliate her, relegate her to her former existence . . . More than once I gave up other things to serve as a substitute audience. For, you see, I had come to realize even then that Maddy and myself were precisely alike; we had learned to bow in order to be loved for our graceless selves.

The encounters with stray dogs—and there are many—go even deeper. Dogs he befriended fifty years ago on a moving train in the West, last year on the street in Philadelphia, yesterday in the ruins of a demolished campus building—one and all are evoked with such power and immediacy that the identification is unmistakable. The dogs are the mongrel in himself, vagrant and at large: a sense of things still very much alive for the accomplished man in his late sixties.

Yet, for all that he cannot or will not address openly, Eiseley never seems either dishonest or withholding. On the contrary, the incapacity is moving. Clearly, the silence within remains a torment and, for him, a living proof of his own oddity. Late in the book he invokes the memory of Edward Blyth, the unsung researcher whose brilliant work Darwin exploited, and whose life—"You, too, were a solitary"—Eiseley resonates to. "Suppose," he writes across the century to Blyth, "we were seated, like the tramps we are, at a fire by the railroad. What would we say as the dark closed in—Men beat men, verbally or physically—is that the most of it?" The sentences lift themselves from the page; beneath them we feel Eiseley's lasting sense of marginality. The final chapters are remarkable.

Coming close to the present, it seems suddenly to matter that he hasn't known what to make of himself as a human among humans. At his mother's funeral, he pleads inarticulately with his wife of forty years—a woman to whom he refers not more than three times in passing, and only once by name—to reassure him that they have, indeed, come "the whole way." She does as she's asked, but her words are of no use to him. In his anxiety, he drives his language on, making it swell fantastically, as though to insist on his allegoric relation to the universe: we now have talking cats, giant wasps, mythic struggles in a blinding, primeval snowstorm.

Abruptly, Eiseley pulls himself together. In a satchel his mother bequeathed him, he finds a huge forgotten bone from his early diggings, an ice-age bison forelimb that now sits on his desk. He lifts the bone, meditates on it and, at the very last, tells us that what*ever* the conflicts have been about, this much he knows, "I did not care for taxonomic definitions, that was the truth of it. I did not care to be a man, only a being." And we believe him. We believe him because we have spent the last few hundred pages in the company of a man whose struggle with himself has been much in evidence (it's the struggle that makes him a trustworthy narrator), and even more in evidence his courage. It's the courage that makes the book.

Loren Eiseley was a man who opened his eyes nearly every morning of his life into a vast and etherizing depression ("a tale of desolations," indeed). Then he swung his legs over the side of the bed, stood up, walked across the room, sat down at the desk and began to work ("in that widening ring of human choice chaos and order renew their symbolic struggle"). That, I believe, is the "find" of the excavator who dug as deep as he could, came up with all that he knew and all that he would not know, and offered it to the reader out of a hard-won understanding that to shape a piece of experience is to hold back the chaos. That extraordinary effort is what we call self-creation.

Randall Jarrell:
Reading To Save His Life

RANDALL JARRELL (BORN IN 1914) IS
easily the most beloved of his generation of
literary critics—the one that includes Lionel
Trilling, Edmund Wilson, and Irving Howe.
He is set apart from the others by the directness
with which he addresses the common reader,
as a friend and an equal, the wonderfully con-
fiding manner implying, "Oh, but you know
all this already, don't you? I'm just writing to
remind you of what you already know." It was
through this belief in, and love of, the common reader that Jarrell found his way into his
strongest writing. It is important that he was a
poet himself—that he knew in the flesh what

it meant to actually make literature—but it is not in the poetry that one experiences Jarrell vibrating with response, it is in the critical essays; essays that are infused with a mysterious, glowing strength imparted by a writer who had himself been, most supremely, a reader. Whatever else he was—poet, husband, southerner, teacher, translator, champion talker, and serious music-lover—it was in the country of book-reading that Randall Jarrell came into his giftedness, moved freely, breathed deeply, reached out from the center to touch the borders of a territory he could truly call his own.

Jarrell once said that without literature human life was animal life. By literature, he meant, equally, both the writing of books and the reading of them. Reading, Jarrell thought, gave us back ourselves in a way that no other kind of non-material nourishment could match. In the ordinary dailiness of life we are alone in our heads, locked into a chaos of half-thoughts, fleeting angers, confused desires. When you read, the noise in your head clears out. You start having full thoughts. Full thoughts begin an internal conversation. Pretty soon, there are two of you in the room: you and your responding self. Now, you've got company, you're connected. No longer do you feel alienated, not from yourself, not from others. Reading, therefore, is a supremely civilizing act.

To read Jarrell's essays is to find oneself in the presence of a man one can *see* reading—the books everywhere, the pencil perpetually in hand—inside the house, outside the house, in the bedroom, the garden, the car, at school, on the tennis court, in the classroom; a man who reads for the sake of reading, a man who is perpetually in the presence of the one book that is waiting to be found by *him*: its ideal respondent.

Robert Lowell said famously of Randall Jarrell, "Randall was the only man I have ever met who could make other writers feel their work was more important to him than his own." And indeed, Jarrell once wrote that it was not his poems, but poetry that he wanted people to read. If they would read Rilke and Yeats and Hardy, he "could bear to have his own poems go unread forever." These words are often quoted as an example of Jarrell's selflessness but, in fact, they are the words of a man speaking out of the deepest self; the words not of a critic, not even of a writer, but of one devoted to the act of making literature because it leads to reading. It was a world of reading that Jarrell wanted to inhabit, a world where there would be no talk about how "difficult" contemporary poetry is because "if we were in the habit of reading poets their obscurity would not matter; and, once we are out of the habit, their clarity does not help." Jarrell wanted reading to become as elemental as air and food.

So you can see how such a man would have hated, absolutely *hated*, the growing professionalization after World War II of literary criticism—that is, the criticism of intellectuals and academics whose relation to reading he, Jarrell, had come to consider instrumental. They read, he said, not to nourish their inner lives but to have opinions, and to make careers. They read systematically, purposefully, excludingly, and they were more interested in each other's opinions of the books than in the books themselves. If, at a literary party, he wrote in 1952:

> you talked about the writings of some minor American novelist or short story writer or poet . . . your hearers' eyes began to tap their feet almost before you had finished a sentence . . . But if you talked about what the ten thousandth best critic in the country had just written, in the last magazine, about the next-worse critic's analysis of *The Ambassadors*, their eyes shone, they did not even interrupt you.

Out of the negative passion this cultural development aroused in him, Jarrell wrote memorably—in pieces like "The Age of Criticism," "The Obscurity of the Poet," "The

Taste of the Age"—to remind the reader of why writers actually write. At the end of one of his celebrated essays on Robert Frost, he tells us that for him Frost's poems never seem to be things made of words, but "things made out of lives and the world that the lives inhabit." These essays on Frost are unforgettable, not so much for the critical analyses embedded in them as for the beauty of Jarrell's own responsiveness: the care and patience and delicacy with which he reads and rereads the poems, making the case each step of the way for Frost being "that rare thing, a complete or representative poet, and not one of the brilliant partial poets who do justice, far more than justice, to a portion of reality, and leave the rest of things forlorn."

One of the most endearing examples of Jarrell's live relation to reading is provided by his argumentative return again and again to the work of poets like Lowell, Wallace Stevens, Marianne Moore, and W. H. Auden. In these pieces he is writing to, as much as about, fellow poets, and he is fervent, a true religious who does not hesitate to speak sternly, even curtly, to the brethren. He loves, analyzes, and rebukes them all at once. His is the conditional adoration of the true reader. Supposedly, Jarrell, angered by what he thought a less than perfect collection, reviewed negatively a new book of Auden's in language of such reckless outrage that Auden crowed, "Oh! Randall is in love with me!"

Among those to whose work he returned often was William Carlos Williams. When Book I of "Paterson" was published in 1946, Jarrell wrote that it seemed to him the best thing Williams had ever done. As time went on, he liked each of the subsequent volumes of Williams's famous poem less and less—and said so, in his energetically violent way. But years later, in an introduction to the "Selected Poems," he writes as though discovering the poet for the first time:

Williams's attitude toward his people is particularly admirable: he has neither the condescending, impatient, Pharisaical dismissal of the illiterate mass of mankind, nor that manufactured, mooing awe for an equally manufactured Little or Common Man, that disfigures so much contemporary writing. Williams loves, blames, and yells despairingly at the Little Men just as naturally and legitimately as Saint-Loup got angry at the servants: because he *feels*, not just says, that the differences between men are less important than their similarities.

Throughout his life, Jarrell was made uneasy that he wrote criticism so fluently and so influentially—he had wanted above all to be a great poet—yet he had the courage not only to not deny his talent, but to realize that this work aroused the same sort of vulnerability that one experienced when making original art. The real critic, he observed more than once, is just as alone with himself as is the poet or novelist, "he can never forget that all he has to go by, finally, is his own response." To be effective, he too, must strip down to "a terrible nakedness."

In his person, Jarrell was as complicated and disordered as his prose was simple and lucid. He was exhibitionist in his dress, overbearing in his excitability, child-like in his loves. Alternately fey, manic, or malicious, for many he was an enchanting, exasperating creature who seemed to take boundless delight in being alive. Yet at the last, some awful darkness reached through the bright composition to yank at him, and in what seemed like no time at all Jarrell spiraled into out-of-control anxiety. In 1963, as he was turning fifty, he went into an extraordinary depression, one that required treatment. After that, it was one long round of drugs, mood swings of frightening extravagance, and repeated hospitalizations. On the evening of Oct 11, 1965, once more under institutional restraint, Jarrell left the hospital without permission, began walking along a road that led in the direction of home, and was sideswiped by a car and killed. The death was judged accidental, but many believed, and still believe, that his recklessness was suicidal. He was mourned intensely by the entire English-speaking literary world.

Two things we know about Jarrell from letters and hospital records and the melancholy memories of his widow: he brooded endlessly on the question of how one was to experience life, and he obsessed over growing old. Experience, as he understood it, depended upon engagement with other people. For that, he realized, one must know oneself; without self-knowledge one could neither know nor be known. To live and die unknown was not to have lived at all.

But the formidable charge that he "know himself" seemed to induce in him only a useless kind of existential terror and, as time passed, he hid from it in a manic enthusiasm for child-like behavior; a pronounced anxiety at being left alone (throughout his marriage his wife was glued to his side); and a recurrent need to write poems in the speaking voices of aging women with whom he was clearly fascinated. In short: the obsessing got him nowhere. He was looking in all the wrong places for the information that was needed.

With hindsight, it seems almost a given that when he passed out of youth into middle age, the terrors would only increase. After fifty, he was made frantic by the sight of himself in the mirror: that creature who stared back at him, growing ever more unrecognizable each year, as the smooth familiarity of an unlined face was steadily consumed by one that threatened a maturity Jarrell could not recognize as anything but alien. The refusal was so severe, it was bound to end in breakdown. If *he* couldn't recognize this changing self, he reasoned madly, how could anyone else? What did it mean, then, to know and be known? What was there to know? *Who* was there to know? His inner life began to feel like it was evaporating. In his own eyes, he was becoming a man empty of self.

The last of Jarrell's publications before he died was a collection of poems. This book received irritated reviews that accused Jarrell of wanting to retreat forever into a childhood innocence that he had written delightfully of before, but that now wearied. Such longing no longer struck an authentic note for the critics; it seemed a pose, a posture, an attitude. In one especially damning review, the exasperated critic accused Jarrell of telltale sloppy writing. The work, he said, was full of unacceptable approximations that revealed a poet often not involved enough in the writing of poetry to work until he had found the exactly right word.

In a certain way, the essay-poetry divide in Jarrell was the objective correlative to his life. With the poems, he couldn't dive deep enough. With the essays, he showed that he knew exactly what it *meant* to dive deep enough, and that while he himself might not do it, he was ever vigilant that it be done. I think I am safe in saying that if Jarrell's final publication had been a collection of essays—the writing that put him most closely in touch with reading—it would not, could not have received reviews anything remotely like the ones dealt out to the poetry. But the choice cannot have been an accidental one: while reading gave Randall Jarrell his life, in the end it could not save it.

Saul Bellow, Philip Roth, and the End of the Jew as Metaphor

FOR SOME TWENTY-FIVE OR THIRTY years—between the mid-1950s and the early '80s—a single explosive development in our literature made the experience of being Jewish-in-America a metaphor that attracted major talents, changed the language, and galvanized imaginative writing around a western world badly in need of a charge. Its two path-breaking stars—one at the start, the other at the end—were Saul Bellow and Philip Roth, a pair of writers who, in a sense, and each in turn, strong-armed the culture into accommodating the experience.

Not another writer after Roth could lay claim to the metaphor with the demanding savvy that he and Bellow had brought to the enterprise.

In its glory days, Jewish-American writing was an indicator of a cultural shift that a couple of million Americans had thought they'd never live to see: a shift that ushered in a final phase of assimilation for Jews at levels of American life previously unavailable to them. It was welcomed half a century ago with a violent rush of words that announced the arrival of a narrating voice whose signature traits were a compulsive brilliance, an exuberant nastiness, and a take-no-prisoners humor edged in self-laceration. These traits never deserted the work of those years; they were in fact, integral to the entire undertaking.

An angry fever inhabited these writers of the '50s and '60s, one that burned with a strength that routinely threatened to either purge or consume the body upon which it fed. Conventional English could not address the

86

condition. What was required was a syntax and a sentence structure that would fan the fever, light up the infection, stimulate a nervous system clearly in distress. The American language was ready to accommodate. Virginia Woolf had once complained that she couldn't find the words to make an English sentence that would describe what illness felt like to her because as an Englishwoman she was constrained from taking liberties with the language. Exactly what outsider literature does in this country: fashions the language anew precisely so that it can express what it feels like to be ill. That, essentially, is what Jewish-American writing at its best has been about. In my view, it would never be about anything else. In the hands of a Saul Bellow or a Philip Roth, such expressiveness could—and did—explode a literary charge of epic dimensions.

They were thoroughly at one with their "illness"—that is, their newfound arrogance over having been marginalized—these Jewish-

American writers of the '50s and '60s, closing the gap between author and narrator to a degree not before seen in American literature. At the heart of the enterprise lay an essence of self-regard that made the writing rise to unmatched levels of verbal glitter and daring, even as its dangerously narrowed scope ruled out sympathy, much less compassion, for any character on the page other than the narrator himself. Most especially was sympathy denied those closest to the narrator, the people he purportedly knew best: friends, family, lovers—particularly lovers; these, if anything, acted only as a foil for the narrator's biting sense of insult and injury. Saul Bellow once said to his biographer, "I had no idea that our moment would be so short." The wonder is not that the moment was short, but that it lasted as long as it did, and created so much influential prose out of so limited a sense of human empathy.

Theirs was a magnificent instance of writers and a time well met. Postwar American literature—from the Beats to Norman Mailer to the Man in the Gray Flannel Suit—was ripe for declarations of insult and injury. What, after all, had it meant to have won the war only to be living inside the straitjacket of Cold War anxiety? Jewish-American writing, with its own scores to settle, was happy to join in the indictment, but, really, its huge success, what an irony it was. Behind that singular forward thrust—beginning with the publication of *The Adventures of Augie March* in 1953—lay a history of social integration that took so long to complete itself that by the time it did, the bad taste in the mouths of these writers had become toxic. It was this very toxicity that gained them emblematic status in a culture characterized by moral exhaustion and liberationist break-out.

AT THE TURN OF THE TWENTIETH CENtury, if you were a Jewish immigrant it was most unlikely that you thought of the English language as anything other than a tool of survival. Yet a mass of writing in English—mainly melodrama and didacticism—poured out of a vibrant sub-culture. Mixed in among the dross was a small number of novels and stories written with a kind of desperate inventiveness by women and men of sensibility. One of the strongest of these is Anzia Yezierska's 1920 story collection, *Hungry Hearts.* Set on New York's Lower East Side, immersed in the life of the streets, the work is yet precocious, concerned as it is not with documenting social misery but with the idea of an inner life thwarted by self as well as world. Today, these stories can be read as one would an artifact uncovered on an archaeological dig.

Inevitably, in Yezierska's work, whether the narrator speaks in the first person or in the third, the story is divided between the time she announces her "wild, blind hunger" for her own life, and the time she realizes that she is trapped in a repression from which hope of release is dim. There is no subject in Yezierska's writing.

The work is all language: language by the rushing mile; language the writer stops up, cuts off at one length or another, calls a story or a novel but, in fact, is only the ongoing sound of that unleashed voice announcing its overwhelming necessity. Occasionally, there comes a page radiant with clarity and detachment, and the reader takes hope—*now* the story will go forward!—but turn that page and we are heading once more into the hurricane. The performance is astonishing. And all the more so when one realizes that forty years on it will be repeated with infinitely greater sophistication and impact, but not much more detachment or control.

College-educated Jews born of immigrant parents in the United States in the first decades of the twentieth century wanted badly to leave that testifying voice behind. Coming of age in the 1930s, many of this generation felt liberated enough in imagination to think of themselves as Jewish-American rather than simply as Jewish. The tricky thing for the Jews of that generation was how to talk and write American, and not sound like one newly arrived to the culture.

In this context, Delmore Schwartz is to Jewish-American writing as Richard Wright is to African-American writing. He is the writer without whom. The one whose work is the bridge between immigrant writing and the writing that was to become more authentically Jewish-American than his own. Born in Brooklyn in 1913 into a household where more Yiddish than English was spoken, he was an epitome of the *arriviste* generation of Jewish-American intelligentsia. His personality was marked by a tidal wave of brilliant speech that had been formed by immigrant experience merged with the sound of the street, and coming out of the mouth of a man who read Eliot and Pound each morning before breakfast. He saw himself as an alienated Jew who was yet indelibly imprinted with the conviction that to serve the literary culture that had been formed by European modernism was a holy mission. In his writing Schwartz would always be both precocious and reverential: at one and the same time an original and a keeper of the culture.

All his life Delmore Schwartz remembered how much he had suffered "being a Jew at Harvard" when he went off to teach there at the end of the Depression. Cambridge in the '40s was death for Delmore. The patricians in the English Department recoiled from him, and it wasn't so much that he was aggrieved by the rejection he met with, as that the conflict that the rejection aroused in him was damaging: at the same time that he despised the academic mandarins at Harvard, he found himself yearning for their recognition and acceptance, and for this he hated himself. Feeling compromised, he was driven to act out a frantic display of urban Jewish smarts that made him behave outrageously, which of course alienated Harvard all the more. It was only when standing at a bar in Greenwich Village, surrounded by friends and intellectual well-wishers, that he was in the responsive presence he required to feed the writing self he now identified with saving literature from the philistines. This was a crusade of immense chutzpah, one that reflected the speed and urgency with which the Jews of his generation responded to the invitation, however grudging and however partial, to imagine themselves not only partaking of American culture, but of influencing it as well.

It was one of those incendiary periods in social history—the late '30s, early '40s—when, out of the break-up of class stability, there arises a complicated promise of change that is experienced by some as salutary, others as threatening. The Great Depression had brought about an extraordinary leveling of social hierarchies—suddenly, all kinds of people did not know who they were or where they stood—and this interruption of social certainty had released emotional extremity of every kind. Thousands of people remembered the Depression as a time of indiscriminate kindness, and thousands remembered it as a time when a shocking murderousness stalked the land. Out of this agitation came an energetic pathology.

Thus, for American Jews in the '30s and '40s, there was a tepid welcome here and there—more Jews breaking into white collar jobs, the arts, and the professions—right alongside a virulent Jew-hatred that made itself felt at every level of society, from the most sophisticated to the most primitive, and nowhere more than in New York City. Arthur Miller's 1945 novel *Focus* was a frightening but plausible fable of the polite anti-Semitism of corporate Manhattan merging with the Christian Front variant in lower-middle-class Queens. The novel tells the story of an amiably conservative WASP working in a big midtown firm who, in his forties, is suddenly required to wear spectacles. As soon as he puts the glasses on, a startling change occurs in his appearance: he looks Jewish. From there the novel takes off as the protagonist loses his job, is ostracized in the neighborhood, and at last not only threatened but attacked. The book is one long anxiety-provoking read.

Yet agitation was better than stasis. For intellectually ambitious Jews, the door of assimilation had been pushed sufficiently open that (if turned sideways) some of them could walk through, even though just across the threshold stood the natives gazing quizzically, with either thinly disguised distaste or open hostility.

There was only one way for intellectual Jews of these decades to be taken seriously, and that was through the replication in their work of high culture. No intellectual Jew walking through the door of American literary life in the '40s would have dreamed of drawing attention to himself by writing otherwise. The boldness of the literature of the time that engages the issue of anti-Semitism lay in *writing* about Jews; it did not lie in *sounding* like Jews.

When writers like Saul Bellow and Delmore Schwartz sat down to write in the '40s, it was as the self-conscious inheritors of a great literary tradition that as yet demanded a conservative differentiation between the narrator and the author. They were hungry to emulate a wholeness of being between the artist and his culture, these writers from working-class immigrant life who longed passionately to do work of the first order for which they suspected the word "undivided" was key.

Let's stop to appreciate the moment. Here it is the late '40s, early '50s. It's the end of the Second World War, the reality of the Holocaust has not yet been absorbed, the United States is at the height of its glamour and power, and the future seems to belong to all who would claim it. Devotion to the claustrophobic atmosphere of one's own hyphenated experience is at an all-time low. The enthusiasts were outnumbering the skeptics. They had decided to love America: surely America would love them back.

But it was not—and now they began to see that it never had been—a simple matter of American culture extending a warm-hearted, "Come on in, you're welcome here." Such long adversarial relationships as that of the Jews and WASP America have a startling yet perfectly predictable consequence: by the time the door opens, those knocking at it are infected with the poison of self-doubt, a substance more toxic than all the historic humiliations combined. As W.E.B. Du Bois once said of being told repeatedly that one is inferior: "First you laugh. Then you get angry. Then you think, maybe they're right." To which James Baldwin, some thirty years later, added bluntly, "It begins with them hating you, and ends with you hating yourself."

In the late 1950s Leslie Fiedler observed that the Jewish-American novelist had internalized the stereotype of the Jew in American literature. When he sat down to write, he had trouble shaking off the hostile or sentimental images that appeared regularly in the work of gentile writers. It is impossible to overestimate the value of such an insight. In our own time, we see—through the efforts of would-be artists among women, gays, and blacks—how long and hard is the road that must be walked in order to leave behind both testament and stereotype, and arrive at the place where one is able to render the full, free taste of one's actual experience. The Jews, said Fiedler with some bitterness, would become jurists, professors, theatre greats, and corporate heads long before they would occupy the world of serious literature—produce a Dos Passos, a Hemingway, a Faulkner. Even a Steinbeck, a Farrell, or a Penn Warren, he added, he was so angry.

Interestingly enough, there *were* works of gut-level imagination being written by American Jews in the '30s and '40s that were neither generic social realism nor highbrow modernism, but, aimed at the mass market reader, they fell below the radar of serious consideration.

It is startling today to read some of them, and find embedded in their pages the origins of the anti-social wildness that only twenty years later would deliver Jewish-American writing as we know it into Fiedler's Promised Land.

In 1937 a novel called *I Can Get It For You Wholesale* became a runaway best-seller. *Wholesale* traces the year in which a big city garment-district hustler named Harry Bogen completes his apprenticeship as a talented swindler, and moves from amateur to professional—cheating, framing, embezzling—all the while gloating at how smart he is, and how deeply stupid everyone around him is.

Harry Bogen is a kind of guttersnipe not seen before in Jewish-American writing. There is not a page in the book on which Harry is not scheming. Scheming is his life's blood. When he gets what he wants he no longer wants it. It's the *next* thing on his ever growing list that he must have. And that next thing inevitably involves gobbling someone up. A psychic tapeworm is at work in Harry. He must eat others because he himself is being eaten alive from the inside out. But, as very few can sustain thinking of themselves as cannibals, it is necessary to dehumanize those whom one is about to consume. Thus, Harry speaks of everyone—and I mean everyone—he encounters in the vivid epithets that degrade: Jews are kikes and mockies; blacks are niggers; women pots, pussies and bitches; and gentiles get the simple, perpetual sneer *goyim*.

Jerome Weidman's *Wholesale* isn't about a primitive on the make, it is the primitivism itself flung down on the page, talking fast and hard, in your ear and in your face. It's an extraordinary act of mimicry, prefiguring the work of Bellow and Roth in that it is not only voice, all voice, nothing but voice; it's a voice working its way into the reader's ear like a plumber's snake, moving directly and relentlessly, carefully avoiding vital organs like the heart, straight down to the gut.

Harry Bogen is the deracinated Depression itself: survival in a world where, admittedly, all bets are off. For readers of the psychologically (as well as physically) starved '30s, Harry was an anodyne. No matter that he was a predator. Readers loved it that he was eating so well.

Perceived (and rightly so) as a piece of popular fiction powered by vicious daring, *Wholesale* nonetheless isolated a level of Jewish-American angst more murderously unforgiving than had previously been imagined. Ultimately, that angst would irradiate the work of writers who knew how to take the liquid material of infuriated dispossession and harden it into the tempered steel of a weapon. The question—then as now—was: to be used against whom?

IN 1949 SAUL BELLOW, THIRTY-FOUR-YEARS old with two books under his belt (*Dangling Man* and *The Victim*), was living in Paris on a Guggenheim fellowship, and feeling pressured to produce a third book in line with the modernist minimalism that had determined the critical success of the first two. He soon realized that he was harnessed to a novel that his heart was simply not in: the writing felt cramped, the vision received, the connection between himself and his material severely strained. The whole situation made his face ache. Every morning he went off to work at his rented studio as though he were going to the dentist. Then one day the intake of a homely image changed everything. The Paris streets were flushed daily by open hydrants that allowed water to run along the curb, and on this particular morning Bellow noticed a dazzle of sunlight on the water that highlighted its flow. His spirits lifted, and he was made restless rather than depressed. Suddenly there opened up before him the memory of a kid from his boyhood who used to yell out "I got a scheme!" when they were playing checkers, then he recalled this kid's vividly abnormal family, and then the Chicago streets from which they had all sprung like weeds pushing up through concrete. An urge to describe that long-ago life overcame him.

Instantly, the gloom disappeared, the unwanted novel got pushed aside, and Bellow began to write "in a spirit of re-union with the kid who had shouted, 'I got a scheme!'" Soon enough that kid got named Augie March, and around him an astonishing sentence structure began to form itself, one that instead of shaping the character, seemed to release the character; not only release him, but determine the course his adventures would take. Language and subject couldn't chase each other fast enough. Bellow marveled at what was happening. It was as though these stories, these people, this word order had been locked up inside him for a lifetime. In fact, as he said years later of *Augie*, "You might put it that he had been in hock for years; for decades. He and I together had been waiting for an appropriate language. By that language and only that language could he be redeemed."

For the first time in his working life, Bellow felt he owned his own writing. With those remembered rhythms in his ear, that syntax and vocabulary on his tongue—an amalgam of immigrant speech, tabloid reporting, and being told in school that George Washington and Abraham Lincoln were *your* presidents—he could take a deep breath and exhale the poetic, ragged, semi-criminal world full of hungry expectation from which he himself had emerged. This language that was pouring out of him now was not, strictly speaking, English—it was American; *his* American; a language, he laughed, that "was mine to do with as I pleased."

The Adventures of Augie March hit the ground running. The book injected a sense of live movement into an atmosphere shot through with the stagnancy of spirit that was allowing Western literature to live with itself in the wake of the Second World War. Alienation of the self was all very well and good, its intensely new American voice called out, but the fact remained, we were *alive*—alive and still yearning. If anyone could make clear the bottomlessness of human yearning, it was Augie March. Here he was, a first-class hunger artist, pushing his way out of a garishly populated disenfranchisement that was, in its own way, a war zone, to claim his right "to not lead a disappointed life." In 1953 that thought was received, both in Europe and in the States, as a welcome aggression against the reverence for spiritual exhaustion that characterized serious literature of the moment. The aggression lay in the daring of the prose—the unexpected vocabulary, the liberty-taking sentences , the mongrel nature of its highbrow-lowbrow narration—in service, ultimately, to what felt like a piece of rescued wisdom about the meaning (that is, the origins) of a disappointed life.

From the get-go, Augie has told us that he's never seen himself as anything other than a blank slate upon which "life" would write a story. "All the influences were lined up waiting for me," he says. "I was born, and there they were to form me, which is why I tell you more of them than of myself." It hasn't occurred to him until now that this headlong plunge of his toward raw experience might prove paradoxically fateful because he could never realize that he was not only being made by the world, he was himself doing quite a bit of the making. In calculating the human cost of what has been lost, injured, or cast aside as he has moved frantically through the running-event that is his life, Augie at last takes into account a prodigious insufficiency of emotional steadiness within himself. He has not, after all, fled the ghetto in one piece; there's a leak in his own appetite-filled heart. An inability, as Augie himself puts it, to love "reliably" has made him culpable in the accumulation of sorrow laced inescapably not only through his own destiny but, we come to feel along with him, that of all humanity. Never again would a character like Augie March hold the page in a Bellow novel speculating with more gravity than irony, more tenderness than grievance, on the terrible dynamic in human affairs that implicates us all.

For Bellow, the writing of *Augie March* was pure joy. It was the joy that made of his protagonist a character entranced by the surge of life, however painful, within and around him; one proposition in the book never in question is that to live in pursuit of experience, whatever the consequence, is an irreducible value. Yet, almost immediately after *Augie* was written, this naked exultation in life for life's sake began to complicate itself in Bellow's prose, and soon gave way to a tone of voice and an angle of vision that grew steadily more manic than eager, more ironic than open, more brilliant than lyric. With the increase in writing glitter, there grew apace a self-pitying disconnect emanating in ever greater degree from the unchanged (and unchanging) first person narrator who dominated all the books to come. It was very much as though that early joy had stemmed from the appeasement of a prolonged hunger to be oneself that, once achieved, made joy unnecessary to a writer not equipped for it by nature. From here on in, the pleasure would consist in attention paid to the humiliation of having had to be hungry for so long: a tendency that proved consequential as Bellow's writing became concentrated in a view of life that increasingly opened itself to the charge of solipsism.

Over the next thirty years Augie would transmute into Henderson, Herzog, Charlie Citrine: ever more fabled and feverish narrators who come increasingly to experience the world as a place of anxiety rather than promise, and themselves as men of trusting spirit under perpetual siege; pitched relentlessly forward into a universe of monumental angst where all bets are *really* off, and every kind of human threat keeps coming at him: the corporate gangsters who "do" the world, the women who promise and don't deliver, the homegrown fast talkers with pity for none. Everywhere this narrator turns, they're at him, pulling the rug out from under him, while he (year by year, title by title) becomes ever more spellbound by the tumult. Increasingly, all he can do is stand there and be inundated.

It was the inundation—in book after book after book—that came as a literary astonishment, the vividness and the gorgeousness of it, glowing with the force of dazzling, inventive complaint pouring out of the mouth of this manic Jew who had swallowed a library; this betrayed lover of art, history, and women, pining for the return of a civilization whose loss he cannot stop documenting. Early Bellow readers encountered the sheer raciness of the performance—migod, can he really be *doing* this?—with a shivery delight that spoke volumes about a time and a writer well met.

Herzog was the pivotal novel. This is the book that delivers in full the sound of the

Jewish-American narrator (the one no gentile could possibly imitate) in a frenzy of spiritual homelessness, putting in place for all Bellow time the way that the world, instead of fortifying him, just keeps coming at him. Tracing five days in the life of a failed academic whose wife has recently left him for his best friend, the novel tells of how Moses Herzog, mad with disbelief that this humiliation has been visited on him—*him*!—rushes about, obsessing like an Ancient Mariner, writing unsent letters to the living and the dead, going endlessly over the whole sorry story of "the betrayal" with an army of characters that comes his way. This fever of Herzog's *is* the book. He wants to understand—oh God yes, to understand!— what has happened, what has really happened, not only superficially to him alone, but to humanity at large: locally, nationally, globally; historically, culturally, politically.

In the course of this monumental effort to grasp his situation Herzog, in an offhand way, tells the reader that he has been a bad husband and father, a cold, ego-serving lover ("It was his pride that must be satisfied, his flesh got what was left over"), a self-involved friend, a painfully inconsiderate son. These recognitions, however, are not to be taken any more seriously than anything else being speculated on, because the real—the undeniable, unforgivable, criminal—guilt lies with *them*. The wife and the friend who have committed moral homicide on his watch. And actually, we can even more or less forget the friend. It's the wife. The wife who now becomes the object of some of the most talented misanthropy in American literature.

Gradually, Herzog's wife, Madeleine, is presented to the reader as a living embodiment of the kind of evil self-interest that represents a threat to the race itself. A creature of inborn moral deformity, a generic Rosemary's baby, she is, spiritually speaking, a human abortion. When Herzog thinks back on it—and what else is he here for?—he sees that she had lived only to do him in. A "plotting bitch with cold, cold eyes" she had, in fact, been born to do him in.

In time, as Herzog goes on obsessing, he realizes that it isn't just the wife, it's women. All women. The women who exercise with cunning and calculation the powers that have been put into them, and them alone, for the specific purpose of bringing him to his knees. Standing on a train platform in New York's Grand Central Station:

> He saw twenty paces away . . . a woman in a shining black straw hat . . . with eyes that reached him with a force she could never be aware of. Those eyes might be blue, green, even gray—he would never know. But they were bitch eyes, that was certain. They expressed a sort of female arrogance which had an immediate sexual power over him; he experienced it again that very moment—a round face, the clear gaze of pale bitch eyes, a pair of proud legs.

In despair over ever being able to fathom the nature of this, his natural enemy, Herzog cries out at his journal, "Who are they? What do they want? They eat green salad and drink human blood."

Thirty years after the Depression—in the wake of the Second World War, nuclear threat, gray-flannel anxiety, imminent cultural break-out—it is women who are the arch evil in the life of the Jewish-American protagonist. And not just any women, his women. It is *they* who poison the spring of life at which our talented, high-minded narrator would otherwise be drinking happily; they who determine that he will stagger and drop in his prime. How else can he defend himself against such unearned malevolence except by writing this book?

What is the contemporary reader to make of such writing? Today, Moses Herzog sounds more like Harry Bogen than Everyman, with his equally mad take on the world as a place where one either eats or is eaten. We more or less understand Harry B's paranoia, but what, exactly, is it with Moses Herzog, and all the Herzogs to come, as Bellow went on creating book-length descriptions of characters for whom women are agents of mortal threat, incomprehensible punishment, deliberate degradation?

It is painful to have to realize that only as Bellow's place in the world took on greater definition did this live sense of grievance against women flare, rising up from a coldness deep in the psyche that no amount of success could make warm to the prospect of human fellowship. Painful, because the grievance, as such, was conspicuously absent from the earlier work.

Writing *Augie March*, his breakout book, produced in Bellow a benevolence of mood so great that in that novel a striking tenderness is extended toward women and men alike as fellow creatures trapped in an existential misery of which they themselves are the originators. Here, he created a man and a woman equally endowed with emotional frailty, and equally responsible for the moral ignorance with which they, as lovers, destruct. If anything, in *Augie March* it is the woman's greater effort at self-understanding that makes the situation large.

Augie's love for Thea Fenchel is glorious in its extremity. "She made my soul topple over," he tells us. Never before had he been "so taken up with a single human being." In time, however, the heat between them begins to cool, and Augie, himself in perpetual need of adoration, strays. He is surprised when Thea is devastated. Their parting scene is something a reader almost never experiences in Bellow's work: heartbreaking.

In this novel, Bellow knows what every great writer knows: that melancholy makes cowards of us all; that among men and women limitations of the spirit are shared, and emotional incapacity evenly parceled out. After *Augie*, though, when the joy of discovering his own voice was spent, he forgot what he knew. The writing itself grew richer and wilder, even as that old, cold, grievous sense of deprivation ate at him, like a parasite demanding to be fed. In no time at all antagonism between the sexes became the nourishment of choice. It went down like ice cream.

That sense of early affliction, for which meanness between women and men served as assuagement, never reduced its power over Bellow. By definition, it resembled an open wound that refused to close. In time it became obvious that it was in the writer's interest to ensure that the wound would never heal: the animus it produced was too valuable. In Bellow's life this animus apparently spilled itself indiscriminately, resulting in a multitude of estrangements; in the work, however, funneled most efficiently through woman-hating, it fed the writing imagination like nothing else Bellow would ever know.

WITH THE SENSATIONAL PUBLICATION IN 1969 of *Portnoy's Complaint,* it became evident that Philip Roth, eighteen years younger than Bellow, was the son arrived to work the father's ground with an even more alarming sense of outrage. The entrenched love-hate attachment to one's own outsiderness, inextricably linked to the war between the sexes, would now be nailed for all time. If in Bellow misogyny was like bile emanating from a festering wound, in Roth it was lava pouring out of an active volcano.

Yet in the son as in the father, animosity toward women-as-women was something that took time to come into its own. *Good-bye, Columbus*, for example, is remarkably sympathetic toward both of its protagonists, a young man and woman equally drawn by the sexual pleasure they take in one another. Here, it is class difference (he's working class from Newark, she's middle class from Short Hills) that provides both the excitement and the denouement; and although there is not a moment when the narrator is not undercutting his own sentimental feeling (Philip Roth devoid of irony is quite literally unimaginable) the level of mockery and self-mockery is so mild as to seem almost affectionate. On their first date (at a swimming pool) Brenda tells Neil about her nose job. He says, "Let me see if you got your money's worth." She says, "If I let you kiss me would you stop being nasty?" They kiss, and Neil reports:

'I felt her hand on the back of my neck and so I tugged her towards me . . . and slid my own hands across the side of her body and around to her back. I felt the wet spots on her shoulder blades, and beneath them, I'm sure of it, a faint fluttering, as though something stirred so deep in her breasts, so far back it could make itself felt through her shirt. It was like the fluttering of tiny wings. The smallness of the wings did not bother me—it would not take an eagle to carry me up those lousy hundred and eighty feet that make summer nights so much cooler in Short Hills than they are in Newark.'

What is present here—and will eventually disappear entirely from Roth's work—is tenderness for women and men together. With tenderness comes comradeship: Brenda is not necessarily more sympathetic a creature than any other woman in Roth's oeuvre, but her fundamental humanity is not in question. When, close to the end, Neil says to himself, "Who is she? What do I really know of her?" it is not to demonize Brenda, it is to underscore the mystery of sexual love. At the very end, when each is accusing the other of fatal misinterpretation, Neil mourns, "I loved you Brenda, so I cared." Brenda in turn pleads, "I loved *you*." They stare at one another. "Then we heard the tense in which we'd spoken . . . I think Brenda was crying too when I went out the door . . . I knew it would be a long while before I made love to anyone the way I had made love to her."

A long while? How about never?

A decade later, in the Roth novel that equates with *Herzog,* Alex Portnoy of *Portnoy's*

Complaint lies on the analyst's couch and, as though declaring himself an opium eater, describes what he has gradually developed into: the clarified nature of his creator's relation to women-as-women, rather than women as fellow creatures. Speaking of himself in the agitated third-person, Roth's Portnoy confides:

> While everybody else has been marrying nice Jewish girls, and having children . . . what he has been doing is—chasing cunt. And *shikse* cunt, to boot! Chasing it, sniffing it, lapping it, *shtupping* it, but above all, *thinking about it*. Day and night, at work and on the street . . . It makes no difference how much the poor bastard actually gets, for he is dreaming about tomorrow's pussy even while pumping away at today's.

And then Alex gets down to it:

> What I'm saying, Doctor, is that I don't seem to stick my dick up these girls, as much as I

stick it up their backgrounds—as though through fucking I will discover America. *Conquer* America—maybe that's more like it . . . scores to settle, coupons to cash in, dreams to put to rest . . . I want what's coming to me—real American ass! The cunt in country-tis-of-thee! I pledge allegiance to the twat of the United States of America—and to the republic for which it stands: Davenport, Iowa, Dayton, Ohio, Schenectady, New York.

Portnoy's Complaint, even more than *Augie March,* was a book for its time. The novel was experienced, at the end of the outlaw '60s, like a dam bursting its floodgates, letting loose a waterfall of madman hungers and grudges wrapped in a deranging hilarity that, most gorgeous of all, threatened to sweep everything before it. It was not only the rushing force of the prose, but the shock of *Portnoy's* deracinated explicitness—its adoration of the unbridled, the anti-social, the passionately infantile at the heart of things—that fed exuberantly into the spirit of the times. The application of all that excess to the proud, swaggering anxiety of (still!) being Jewish-in-gentile-America—as good a representation as any of all that the liberationist culture hoped to bring to its knees—insured *Portnoy's* success as a landmark work whose literary qualities would forever be confused with the history of its moment. Which, as it happened, included Jewish assimilation as, very nearly, a fait accompli. That, perhaps, was the *real* rub.

Collectively speaking, if we chart the internal mood of every successful movement for social integration we find that, ironically, with each advance actually made, it is anger—not hope, much less elation—that deepens in the petitioners at the gate. Ironic but not surprising: to petition repeatedly is to be reminded repeatedly that one is not wanted, never has been, never will be. Such recognition encourages a strengthening of the ugliest of feelings—which is why, as James Baldwin said, an oppressed people greets the promise of liberation more often as a snarling antagonist than as a gratified suppliant. Even more distressing, the snarling itself, after generations of passivity, feels good, and soon more than good, necessary, a thing in and of itself hard to give up.

In *Portnoy's Complaint,* probably for the first time in Jewish-American literature, woman-hating is openly equated with a consuming anger at what it means to be pushed to the margin, generation after generation. For men like Bellow and Roth, the sense of outrage was so pent-up that it was inevitable not only that it would vent itself on those closest to hand, but that it would confuse them with the powers that be. Beginning with *Herzog* and *Portnoy,* theirs was a literature that screamed "Don't tell *me* I don't run things around here!"—only it was screaming it at the women its authors slept with.

Portnoy was a watershed book; after that, the distance between narrator and author closed with exponential speed, and the resemblance between Roth and Bellow began to take on historic meaning. The more fantastically realized the Roth narrator became, the more celebrated and lionized, loved and rewarded, the more gripped was the creator of his being by angers and grievances that seemed to rise up steadily out of the primeval deep. His impassioned equation of woman-hating with being Jewish-in-America soon outstripped that of his talented elder by a cynical mile, and revealed a temperament even more driven to the edge. Less and less did the misogyny in Roth's work seem a function of character, more and more an indication of the author's own swamped being. In *Portnoy* the reader could still believe that the women are monstrous because Portnoy experiences them as monstrous. In all the books to follow over the next thirty years, the women are monstrous because for Philip Roth women are monstrous.

The pity of it all is the loneliness trapped inside Roth's radiant poison. In *The Anatomy Lesson* (by now it's 1983) Nathan Zuckerman cries out, "How have I come to be such an enemy and a flayer of myself? And so alone! Oh, so alone! Nothing but *self*! Locked up in *me*!" For Zuckerman, life, from beginning to end, is a howling wilderness. He is alone on the planet: alive but in solitary. All he has ever had to keep him company is the sexual force of his own rhetoric. Unchanged and unchanging, he struggles on, book after book, decade after decade, doomed to repeat in language that glows in the dark the increasingly tired narrative of the illness from which he can neither recover nor expire: his solipsism. He has succumbed to the danger inherent in closing the space between author and narrator; he has fallen in love with the inability to see himself in anyone other than himself, a development that leads inexorably to stasis.

Ten years ago, Philip Roth, realizing that this material in its unreconstructed form had been sucked dry, suddenly and without warning, with the publication of *American Pastoral,* abandoned it, thus bringing Jewish-American writing at what had been its richest and most significant to an unceremonious close.

ROTH'S WAS THE LAST GENERATION OF American Jews to be born into the hyphenated existence. Thereafter, the parents of American Jews were also American. The claim on existential outsiderness that, from its inception, had acted as a foundation for Jewish-American writing was, almost overnight, a thing of the past. No longer would the useful neurosis that marked those who'd grown up half in, half out of the culture be grounded in first-hand experience. After that, if an American Jew felt him or herself a born outsider, it was a personal problem, not a metaphor.

During this same period of time that immigrant parents were disappearing from the lives of American Jews—the 1960s and '70s—relations between women and men were undergoing the historic change that was largely responsible for the erosion of complicity between Bellow and Roth and their readers. It was the women's movement, more even than completed assimilation, that revealed the displacement behind all that trademark ˉmisogyny. As the social reality of Jewish outsiderness waned, the brilliant fever at the heart of Jewish-American writing began to lose its natural source of energy. This turn of events delivered an unexpected piece of information about the entire enterprise. The work was inextricably bound up not so much with being kept out, as with the sickness of *feeling* kept out. Woman-hating had been the synthetic source of energy that was needed to keep the *sense* of "illness" alive. Without that, the work had nowhere much to go, and nothing much to say.

In the nineteenth century Jewish mockery was described by a critic of Yiddish literature as "the sick despair of those for whom life is a permanent witticism." It would never get beyond the limited force of its own excoriating humor. That force could hold everyone and everything up to superior ridicule, but it could not penetrate its own self-deceptions; hence, it could not deepen psychologically. If you accept this observation as a given—and I do—you cannot help wondering how much of *ur*-Bellow and Roth will prove to have transcended its moment of cultural glory. Somehow, it is hard to imagine yesterday's savaging brilliance transmuting into tomorrow's wisdom.

Allen Ginsberg:
America's Holy Fool

THE DAY AFTER ALLEN GINSBERG'S
celebrated 1955 reading of *Howl* in San Francisco, the publisher of City Lights Books sent
Ginsberg a telegram that read, "I greet you at
the beginning of a great career"—the phrase
that Emerson had used, writing to Whitman
upon the publication, exactly a hundred years
earlier, of *Leaves of Grass.* Fifty years on, I think
it can safely be agreed upon that Allen Ginsberg
is the U.S. poet who, within living memory,
most legitimately resembles Whitman. He,
like Whitman, wrote an emblematic American
poem that became world famous; was experienced pre-eminently as a poet of the people,

at home among the democratic masses; and developed a public persona to match the one in his writing: that of the open-hearted, spiritually talented, self-promoting exhibitionist. He is also, again like Whitman, remembered as a man in possession of an extraordinary sweetness that, throughout his life, welled up repeatedly to astonish the hearts of all who encountered him.

I met Ginsberg only twice, the first time at Jack Kerouac's funeral in 1969. I was there for the *Village Voice.* It was my first assignment as a working journalist. Here is the scene as I remember it:

At the head of the viewing room stood the casket with Kerouac, hideously made up, lying in it. In the mourners' seats sat Kerouac's middle-class, French-Canadian relatives—eyes narrowed, faces florid, arms crossed on their disapproving breasts. Around the casket— dipping, weaving, chanting *Om*— were Allen Ginsberg, Peter Orlovsky, and Gregory Corso.

Then there was Kerouac's final, caretaker wife, a woman old enough to be his mother, weeping bitterly and looking strangely isolated. I sat mesmerized, staring in all directions. Suddenly, Ginsberg was sitting beside me. "And who are you?" he asked quietly. I told him who I was. He nodded, and wondered if I was talking to people. Especially the wife. I must be sure to talk to her. "Oh, no," I said quickly. "I couldn't do *that*." Ginsberg nodded into space for a moment. "You must," he murmured. Then he looked directly into my eyes. "It's your job," he said softly. "You must do your job."

The second time we met, nearly twenty years later, was at an infamous meeting of the PEN Board called to debate a letter (drafted by Ginsberg) that the Freedom-to-Write Committee had sent to Israel's premier, taking his government to task for censoring Palestinian and Israeli journalists. I sat in my seat, listening to Ginsberg read his letter aloud to a packed room. He was now in his sixties, his

133

head bald, his beard trim, wearing an ill-fitting black suit, the voice as gentle as I remembered it and twice as dignified. Although the letter had been signed by Susan Sontag, William Styron, and Grace Paley among others, it was Ginsberg himself who drew fire from the opposition. In a communiqué that had been sent earlier to the Committee, Cynthia Ozick had practically accused him of being an agent for the PLO, and now, the essence of the charge coming from the floor seemed to be, "It's people like you who are destroying Israel." I remember Ginsberg standing there, his glasses shining, nodding in all directions, urging people toward compassionate reason. He never raised his voice, never spoke with heat or animosity, never stopped sounding thoughtful and judicious while all about him were losing their heads. When he stepped from the microphone and was making his way through the crowd, I pressed his hand as he passed me and thanked him for the excellence of the letter's prose. He stopped, closed his other hand over mine and, looking directly into my eyes, said softly, "I know you. Don't I know you? I *know* you."

ALLEN GINSBERG WAS BORN IN NEWARK, New Jersey in 1926 to Louis and Naomi Ginsberg. The father was a published poet, a high school teacher, and a socialist; the mother an enchanting free spirit, a passionate communist, and a woman who lost her mental stability in her thirties. Ultimately, she was placed in an institution and lobotomized. Allen and his brother grew up inside a chaotic mixture of striving respectability, left-wing bohemianism, and certifiable madness in the living room. It all felt *large* to the complicated, oversensitive boy who, discovering that he lusted after boys, began to feel mad himself and, like his paranoid parents, threatened by, yet defiant of, the America beyond the front door.

None of this accounts for Allen Ginsberg; it only describes the raw material that, when the time was right, would convert into a bohemian hedonism of mythic proportion that merged brilliantly with its moment: the complicated aftermath of the Second World War characterized by atomic-bomb anxiety, a manipulated terror of godless communism, the strange pathos of the Man in the Gray Flannel Suit, and the subterranean currents of romanticized lawlessness into which the men and women ultimately known as the Beats would funnel an old American devotion to the idea of revolutionary individualism.

When Ginsberg entered Columbia University in 1943 he was already possessed of a presentation of self, shall we say, that would make it impossible for him to gain the love of the teachers he most admired; namely, Lionel Trilling and Mark Van Doren, both socially conservative keepers of academic high culture. (Trilling memorialized Ginsberg in his short story *Of This Time, Of That Place* as the brilliant student whom the academic narrator can experience only as mad.) To emulate these men would mean going into a kind of internal exile that Allen, even then, knew he could not sustain. His dilemma seemed profound. Then he met Jack Kerouac, also a student at Columbia. Through Kerouac he met William Burroughs; together they picked up a Times Square junkie poet named Herbert Huncke; and after that Neal Cassady, the wild man of all their dreams: a handsome, grown-up delinquent who drank, stole, read Nietzsche, fucked like a machine, and drove great distances at great speeds for the sake of movement itself. As Burroughs put it, "Wife and child may starve, friends exist only to exploit for gas money, Neal must move." (Cassady became Dean Moriarty in *On the Road* and the Adonis of Denver in *Howl*.)

For Ginsberg, these new friends soon came to constitute a sacred company of inspired madmen destined, through their writing, to convert the poisoned atmosphere of America's cold war politics into one of restored beauty.

Allen himself—prowling the streets of New York in the late 1940s as if it were Dostoevsky's Petersburg; rising in class at Columbia to terrify both students and teachers alike with some extraordinary, unpunctuated rant; looking for sex in Times Square; seeing Blake in a vision in his own kitchen; nodding wordlessly when the cops ask him if he is a homosexual—seems an emblematic figure standing squarely in the foreground of national disconnect.

The conviction among them of literary destiny was powerful. And why not? People like Ginsberg, Kerouac, and Cassady are born every hour on the hour: how often do their lives intersect with a political moment that endows their timeless hungers with the echoing response of millions, thereby persuading them that they are, indeed, emissaries of social salvation? What was remarkable among this bunch—considering how much they drank, got stoned, and flung themselves across the country in search of heavenly despair—was how well this sense of destiny sustained them throughout their faltering twenties, when life was all worldly rejection and self-dramatizing desperation.

In 1949, now twenty-three years old, depressed and at loose ends, Ginsberg let Herbert Huncke—a true criminal—crash at his apartment. There Huncke proceeded to stash an ever increasing amount of stolen goods. Inevitably, the police appeared at the door, and everyone was arrested. Rescued from a prison sentence by friends, family, and his Columbia teachers, Ginsberg was sent to the New York State Psychiatric Institute where he spent eight months that did, indeed, change his life. Here he met the man to whom he would dedicate *Howl*.

Carl Solomon was Allen's double—a Bronx-born, bisexual, self-dramatizing, left-wing intellectual. They saw themselves in one another almost immediately. Solomon held out his hand and said, "I'm Kirilov (a character in Dostoevsky's *The Possessed*). Allen responded, "I'm Myshkin" (Dostoevsky's fabled *Idiot*). There was, however, one important difference between them. Solomon had lived in Paris, was soaked in existentialist politics and literature, and here, at New York Psychiatric, he introduced Allen to the work of Genet, Artaud, and Celine: the mad writers with whom he instantly felt at one. Ginsberg marveled at Solomon's melancholy brilliance, and proceeded to mythicize it. If Carl was mad, it could only be that Amerika had driven him mad. When Ginsberg emerged from the institution he had his metaphor in place: "I saw the best minds of my generation destroyed by/ madness, starving hysterical naked/ dragging themselves through the negro streets at dawn/ looking for an angry fix."

For the next few years he wandered all over the country and half around the world, becoming a practicing Buddhist along the way. Arrived at last in San Francisco in 1954 (with Kerouac, Cassady, and Corso dancing about him), here and now, in the American city experienced as most open (that is, farthest from the seats of Eastern power), he wrote his great poem, read it aloud one night in October of 1955—and awoke to find himself famous.

While thousands of young people responded to *Howl* as though they'd been waiting years to hear this voice speaking these words, the literary establishment promptly vilified it. Trilling hated the poem, John Hollander hated it, James Dickey hated it, and Norman Podhoretz hated it. Podhoretz hated it so much that he wrote about it twice, once in the *New Republic* and then again in *Partisan Review.* By the time these pieces were being written, *On the Road* had been published, as well as *Naked Lunch,* and for Podhoretz the American sky was falling. The Beats, he said, were the barbarians at the gate, rabble-rousers who "embraced homosexuality, jazz, dope-addiction and vagrancy" (he got that part right), at one with "the young savages in leather jackets who have been running amuck in the last few years with their switch-blades and zip guns." Jack Kerouac was cut to the quick, and wrote to complain that the Beats were about *beatitude* not criminalism; they were here to *rescue* America from corporate death and atomic bomb politics, not destroy her.

In the summer of 1957 *Howl* was brought to trial in San Francisco on charges of obscenity, with a wealth of writers testifying on behalf of the poem's literary value. In retrospect, the trial can now be seen as an opening shot in a culture war destined to throw long shadows across American life. And indeed, throughout the '60s, both the poem and its author were celebrated, the former as a manifesto of the counter-culture, the latter as one of its iconic figures.

Today, more than fifty years after it was written, *Howl* is never out of print, is read all over the world (it's been translated into more than two dozen languages), and by most standards is considered a literary classic. Like *Leaves of Grass,* it is an ingenious experiment with the American language that did what Ezra Pound said a great poem should do: make the language new. Its staccato phrasing, its mad juxtapositions and compacted images, its remarkable combining of the vernacular with the formal—obscene, slangy, religious, transcendent, speaking now in the voice of the poet, now of the hipster—is simply an astonishment. The effect of all this on the reader? "Even today," as one of Ginsberg's biographers says, "reading the poem yields a feeling of intoxication. The words produce an electrical charge that is exhilarating."

GINSBERG ALONE, AMONG THE MAJOR Beat figures, proved a man of emotional genius. Kerouac, Corso, Burroughs, each had a leak somewhere in the middle of himself that made experience drain exhaustingly away; in none of them could either the life or the work mature; all remained trapped in the idiom of

143

the youthful rebel. Ginsberg, however, taught himself to inhabit the ritualized values of his Beat beginnings (especially that of "beatitude") so brilliantly and so insistently that, at last, he made of them, in his own person, a lasting cultural presence.

Like Whitman, he dramatized himself as a person chosen for enlightenment. After he had seen Blake in his kitchen, he said, "I began noticing in every corner where I looked evidences of a living hand, even in the bricks, in the arrangement of each brick. Some hand placed them there—some hand had placed the whole universe in front of me." He now had special sight: he could look at people, and see right through to the essence of their lives. With special sight came the ecstasy of compassion.

The ecstasy, however, came and went, returning only periodically and usually only when drug-induced. In search of permanent exaltation, Ginsberg undertook to spend years of his life meditating on an idea of compassion that the Beats had charged American culture with denying them. Such compassion would, of necessity, be pantheistic in nature, all that lived and breathed worthy of it. His own life, he determined, would come to mimic this pursuit of oneness—an essence of compassion, so to speak—and the poetry of hedonism would be its objective correlative. His poems, springing up with the same spontaneity with which he so often shed his clothes in public, would be both a record and an embodiment of the organic wisdom flowing from the lived life: at once both active and meditative; saintly and sexual; aesthetic and homely.

So here we have this homosexual son of Jewish lower-middle-class autodidacts, willing himself, in the mid-twentieth century, to an inspired transcendence worthy of Emerson, Wordsworth, Buddha—and to a remarkable degree, achieving it.

For the formal poets and critics of his own generation, Ginsberg would remain only a gifted amateur—in 1963 Robert Lowell wrote to Elizabeth Bishop, "the beats have blown away, the professionals have returned"—but for the culture at large, he would—like Walt Whitman—become an inspirited incarnation: the authentic made-in-America holy fool. No mean feat, as this is an identity it takes a lifetime of dedicated practice to achieve. I don't think it an exaggeration to say that when Allen Ginsberg died at seventy his life had given new meaning to the American devotion to self-creation.

Raymond Carver, Andre Dubus, Richard Ford: Tenderhearted Men

THERE'S A CERTAIN KIND OF AMERICAN story that is characterized by a laconic surface and a tight-lipped speaking voice. The narrator in this story has been made inarticulate by modern life. Vulnerable to his own loneliness, he is forced into an attitude of hard-boiled self-protection. Yet he longs for things to be other than they are. He yearns, in fact, for tender connection. Just behind the leanness and coolness of the prose lies the open but doomed expectation that romantic love saves. Settings vary and regional idioms intrude, but almost always in these stories it is men-and-women-together that is being written about.

Fifty or sixty years ago the strongest version of this story was written by Ernest Hemingway. Today, it survives in the work of Raymond Carver, Richard Ford, and Andre Dubus. One enormous difference obtains between the earlier writer and the later ones. Hemingway held an allegorical view of life that idealized women as the means of spiritual salvation, then condemned them as agents of subversion. Raymond Carver, Richard Ford, and Andre Dubus are neither sexists nor misanthropes. On the contrary: tenderness of heart is their signature trait. These men share an acute sense of the compatriot nature of human suffering. Their women are fellow victims.

Nevertheless, from Hemingway to Andre Dubus, what is striking to a reader like me is the extraordinarily fixed nature of what goes on between characters who are men and characters who are women. The narrator invariably subscribes to an idea of manhood that hasn't changed in half a century, and the women he knows seem to subscribe similarly. Their relations are the irreducible in the writing: a central metaphor for Hemingway's three successors. Men and women struggling together in dumb erotic need arouses in each of these writers an astonishing capacity to respond to the desolation of ordinary lives in modern times. It gives them a strength of despair from which their powers derive. And it leaves me with the taste of ashes in my mouth.

THERE'S A SMALL CARVER STORY CALLED "Are These Actual Miles?" that illustrates perfectly what I mean. Toni and Leo are married. Leo has gone bankrupt. All that remains is the red convertible bought in the good years. Toni is being sent out to sell the car for the best price she can get. She leaves the house, dressed to kill, at four in the afternoon. Leo sits waiting for her return. Just after nine, she calls to say the sale is almost completed. He hears music in the background. "Where are you?" he asks nervously. A bit more conversation, and she hangs up. A while later she calls again: Any minute now, honey. "Come home," he pleads. She hangs up. Two or three hours later, another call. He's frantic. At dawn she comes in drunk, with the check in her purse. He looks at her. "Bankrupt!" she screams, and passes out. Leo puts her to bed. After a while, he gets in beside her. Here are the final lines of the story:

> Presently he reaches out his hand and touches her hip . . . He runs his fingers over her hip and feels the stretch marks there. They are like roads, and he traces them in her flesh. He runs his fingers back and forth, first one, then another. They run everywhere in her flesh, dozens, perhaps hundreds of them. He remembers waking up the morning after they bought the car, seeing it, there in the drive, in the sun, gleaming.

Her stretch marks, his convertible: it comes finally to that. The story, like much of Carver's fiction, is permeated with the nakedness of the moment. This is Carver's great strength: stunning immediacy, remarkable pathos. Few American writers can make a reader feel, as he does, right up against it when a character experiences loss of hope. It is impossible to resist the power of such writing, and while I'm reading the story I don't. But then I find myself turning away. The atmosphere congeals. I feel manipulated. These people fail to engage me. I cannot be persuaded that life between Toni and Leo was good when the convertible stood gleaming in the driveway. What's more, I don't think Carver thinks life was good then, either. I think he yearns to believe that it *should* have been good, not that it actually was. This yearning is the force behind his writing. What fuels the intensity of his gaze, the clarity with which he pares down the description, is not a shrewd insight into the way things actually are between this man and this woman, but a terrible longing to describe things as they might have been—or should have been. The sense of loss here is original and primal, unmediated by adult experience.

Connection between people like Toni and Leo is predicated on the existence of a world in which men and women conform to a romantic notion of themselves as men and women. These two have never been real to each other. They were bound to end in her stretch marks, his convertible. Carver knows that. Instead of being jolted by what he knows, startled into another posture, he feels only sad and bad. He mourns the loss of romantic possibility in each life; story after story—"What Do You Do in San Francisco?" "Gazebo," "They're Not Your Husband," "Little Things." "What We Talk About When We Talk About Love"—is saturated in a wistful longing for an ideal, tender connection that never was, and never can be. Carver's surrogate character seems always to be saying, "Wouldn't it be lovely if it could have been otherwise?" In short: the work is sentimental. Trapped inside that sentimentality is the struggle so many women and so many men are waging now to make sense of themselves as they actually are. The struggle has brought men-and-women-together into a new place; puzzling and painful, true, but new nonetheless. In the country of these stories not only is that place not on the map, it's as though the territory doesn't exist.

THERE'S A NOVEL BY RICHARD FORD IN WHICH the narrating protagonist says:

> Women have always *lightened* my burdens, picked up my faltering spirits and exhilarated me with the old anything-goes feeling though anything doesn't go, of course, and never did . . . [But now] . . . I have slipped for a moment out onto that plane where women can't help in the age-old ways . . . Not that I've lost the old

yen, just that the old yen seems suddenly defeatable by facts, the kind you can't sidestep—the essence of a small empty moment.

Frank Bascombe delivers himself of this insight on page 61 of *The Sportswriter* and then goes on speaking until page 375 exactly as though he hadn't. Taking in his own experience is not what this man is about.

Frank came to New York in his twenties—from an anonymous American life that included Mississippi and the Midwest—because he'd written a book of stories that promised to commit him to a life of literature. But New York terrified him, and he couldn't keep up the writing. So he got married, became a sportswriter, and moved to the suburbs. Frank tells us all this as though he himself is puzzled as to how this drastic turn of events came about. "I had somehow lost my sense of anticipation at age twenty-five," he offers by way of explanation. "And I had no more interest in what I might write next than I cared what a rock weighed on Mars."

It's emblematic of the book that Frank, now thirty-eight and divorced, can't figure out why things have turned out as they have, and finds his own ignorance strange and dreamy. "Dreamy" is his euphemism, the word he uses to describe the way he feels about almost everything: the end of serious writing, the death of his son, the breakup of his marriage, the love affairs that come to nothing. New York saddens him unbearably, and New Jersey gives him rest and relief. Everything else makes him dreamy.

Frank Bascombe's depression is Richard Ford's weakness. Ford is in love with it. It is responsible for the tenderness he bears the men in his stories, nearly all of whom are drifters, pained and bewildered people driven by their own sad emptiness into prototypical American violence. Here, in *The Sportswriter,* Ford has abandoned dialect, so to speak, but the commuter and the drifter are the same man: lonely, confused, hurting. Especially confused. It's the bewilderment that touches Ford deeply. Frank's not knowing what is happening to him is the story Ford is telling—life inflicting itself on the most ordinary of men.

But there is so much Frank Bascombe *could* understand, and seems not to *want* to understand, that it is hard to trust his pain. For example, his perpetual dreaminess about the women in his life is unpersuasive. The novel begins with an affair. Frank tells us that he loves the dating ritual and that Vicki, a nurse from Texas, loves to let him love it. He also tells us that it is in Vicki's nature to put her faith "more in objects than in essences. And in most ways that makes her the perfect companion." Then he tells us that he longs to run away with Vicki, to marry her and bliss out forever on her good-natured sexiness. Ford allows Frank to mock himself, to parody his own expectations of love, but Vicki is so unremittingly a fantasy that this entire episode seems only peculiar. The man who daydreams this kind of rescue is, somehow, not credible.

At the end of the novel, Frank has another affair of a few months' duration, this time with a college girl who spends a summer at the magazine he works for. Toward the end of this one, Frank observes: "I doubt ours is a true romance. I am too old for her; she is too smart for me . . . I . . . have also been pleased to find out she is a modern enough girl not to think that I can make things better for her one way or another, even though I wish I could." Not true. He doesn't wish it at all. It's only errant wistfulness drowsing through him.

Between these two affairs, the novel gives us summarized evocations of other women Frank has slept with, or failed to sleep with. These women are spoken of in the way that we all speak of those who once caused sexual infatuation to bloom in us: not as people who are real in themselves, reminders only of the aliveness we have felt in passion.

It is inconceivable in *The Sportswriter* that a person who is a woman should strike Frank simply as a familiar: another human being floating around in the world, lost, empty, shocked to the bone by the way it's all turned out. The only female character in the book who even comes close is his ex-wife, and she, incredibly enough, is called X. It is X who brought on the divorce, X who found the emptiness between them unbearable, X who wanted to take another stab at living her life and, although she looks like a busy suburban mother, X, too, seems to be floundering and suffering. We can only deduce this from the hints Frank throws out. We never see X straight on. She is a a shadowy figure, always at the periphery of Frank's vision. One would assume that he would know her well. But he doesn't. She is just the ex-wife. He feels compassion for women but not empathy; at bottom, they do not remind him of himself. In his mind, the people who embody his condition are other men he runs up against in a random fashion. There are these men, who are like himself, and then there are the women, who can no longer give comfort against the overwhelming force of life.

ANDRE DUBUS, THE MOST COMPLEX AND least well known of the three, is the most articulate in the matter of men-and-women-together. A writer who yearns for Roman Catholicism, loves the Marines, and suffers over the loss of permanence in marriage, Dubus makes the metaphor reach with as much ambition as did Hemingway. His stories and novellas are filled with this preoccupation. It runs like a continuous current beneath the surface of his prose, providing his work with force and direction, and sometimes taking the work down to a place where the waters are still, and very deep indeed. His is among the strongest writing in American fiction. The strength both compels and disturbs, as the work describes with transparency a condition of life it seems, almost self-consciously, to resist making sense of.

Dubus's characters—blue-collar people who live in the old mill towns not far from Boston—are mechanics, waitresses, bartenders, and construction workers. They have almost no conversation in them, and very little sense of things beyond their immediate needs. They drink, they smoke, they make love: without a stop. Inevitably, the limitation of appetite becomes apparent, and they begin to suffer. When they suffer, they do terrible things to themselves, and to one another. There is nothing any of them can do to mitigate the suffering. They cannot educate themselves out of their lives, they can't leave home, and they can't get reborn. This situation is Dubus's subject, the thing he concentrates on with all his writer's might. His concentration is penetrating. We feel his people trapped in their lives so acutely that they enter into us.

The sympathetic detachment he brings to bear on the failure of marriage to lessen the emptiness of soul lying in wait for his characters is Dubus's strongest quality. It is there in some of his best work: in the novel *Voices From the Moon*, as well as in the novellas *Adultery* and *We Don't Live Here Anymore*, where the working class is deserted for a set of characters drawn from Dubus's own life. But working class or middle class, the people in these stories all suffer relentlessly from the same terrible surprise. It is the surprise one feels most vividly. This failure of marriage has been a central experience for Dubus, one that seems to have come unexpectedly and with a jolt. The shock and the immensity of it remain with him.

In *Adultery*, Hank and Edith meet as graduate students in Iowa. He's serious, she's not. He works passionately to make himself a writer; she only wants to be the girl he loves. They marry, have a child, and for Edith the years pass in contentment. Hank, meanwhile, is being eaten up by his life: he grows hungrier by the day, restless and ambitious for he knows not what. He begins an affair. Edith faces him down. He denies nothing. In fact, he tells her he doesn't believe in monogamy. She is astonished and frightened. "Why didn't I ever know any of this," she says. "You never asked," he replies. He tells her to calm down; he says he loves her and wants to continue as a family. Only now, he adds, things are out in the open; there's no going back to their old way of being together. Edith is stricken, but she feels helpless. She agrees to an openly adulterous marriage: he will have lovers, she will have lovers. Five years pass. Then Edith takes as a lover a forty-year-old man who has just left the priesthood. She's the only woman Joe Ritchie has ever slept with. Joe is shocked by her marriage. He tells her she is living in sin, and if she stays with Hank she'll "grow old in pieces." Slowly, she comes to see her life as her lover sees it. Within the year, Joe begins to die of cancer. Edith nurses him. Now, as he nears death, she is repelled by her marriage. She tells Joe she is divorcing her husband.

The genius lies with having given the story to Edith: it is from inside her thoughts and feelings that we read. She—the untried, girlish woman—is the blank slate on which to write the grief, rage, and humiliation of modern marriage. It is Edith who will best register the cost to the human spirit, Edith who can instruct the reader in what it feels like to make an unholy alliance, Edith who makes your skin crawl.

Adultery is not a plea for the return of old-fashioned monogamous marriage; it is only a description of one kind of spiritual hell. Because marriage means so much to Dubus, he is able to use its corrupted form to describe the dictates of the human heart under vile circumstances in perilous times. This novella is his masterpiece. It is also a blueprint for his fundamental text on men-and-women-together.

There is a scene in *Adultery* in which Edith observes her husband at a party. Here's a bit of what she's thinking:

Edith watched Hank, and listened to him. Early in their marriage she had learned to do that. His intimacy with her was private; at their table and in their bed they talked; his intimacy with men was public, and when he was with them he spoke mostly to them, looked mostly at them, and she knew there were times when he was unaware that she or any other woman was in the room. She had long ago stopped resenting this; she had watched the other wives sitting together and talking to one another; she had watched them sit listening while couples were at a dinner table and the women couldn't group so they ate and listened to the men. Usually men who talked to women were trying to make love with them, and she could sense the other men's resentment at this distraction, as if during a hand of poker a man had left the table to phone his mistress. Of course she was able to talk at parties; she wasn't shy and no man had

ever intentionally made her feel he was not interested in what she had to say; but willy-nilly
they patronized her. As they listened to her she
could sense their courtesy, their impatience for
her to finish so they could speak again to their
comrades . . . [She saw that] Hank needed and
loved men, and when he loved them it was
because of what they thought and how they
lived. He did not measure women that way;
he measured them by their sexuality and good
sense. He and his friends talked with one another because it was the only way they could
show their love . . . It no longer bothered her.
She knew that some women writhed under
these conversations; they were usually women
whose husbands rarely spoke to them with the
intensity and attention they gave to men.

In Dubus's work, sexual love is entirely instrumental. Men and women are alive to themselves and to one another only in the mythic
way. They provoke in themselves the fantasy
that romantic love will bring one to safe haven.

They are tremendously influenced by an idea of "men" and an idea of "women" that Ernest Hemingway would have understood and approved of, but that many people today find alarming, if not downright silly. The reader can see early on that the marriage in *Adultery* will come to disaster. Without genuine connection—that is, connection of the mind or spirit—sexual feeling quickly wears itself out. Such love is bound to come a cropper. Yet neither Dubus nor his characters see what the reader sees. In many of his stories, the characters are middle-aged and have been through these affairs many times over. Yet they remain devoted to the fantasy. They resist taking in their own experience. Theirs is the distress of people unable to arrive at wisdom.

Behind Hank and Edith (and Hank's future girlfriends) stand the young men and women in Dubus's Marine stories and his loss-of-virginity stories. Here young men elevate the mystique of physical courage into an idea of manhood that today seems puzzling, and young women develop a concern for virginity that is equally off-putting. Even if the models for these stories still exist—and, of course, they do, in the tens of thousands—they are, in some large sense, no longer plausible. They seem to occur in a vacuum of history. What Dubus has to say in these stories is so emotionally unconvincing that, even though he writes the same good prose he always does, and one reads every sentence with interest, the work loses power.

To create characters who are themselves unknowing is one thing; to write as though you know only as much as your characters know is another. In these stories, there is no distance at all between character and narration. Dubus seems to be at one with these young men and women. He is soaked in nostalgia, even as they are, for an idea of men-and-women-together that is evaporating now—and, for many of us, can't dry up fast enough.

But Dubus doesn't want that idea to go. When we get to his Catholicism, we see how deeply he does not want it to go, and we see even more clearly what lies behind the poetic toughness of his writing.

In "A Father's Story" we have a man speaking from the middle of his life. He's divorced, a devout Catholic who will not remarry; he lives alone on a horse farm, his only friend the local priest. Slowly, he tells us about last summer, when his twenty-year-old daughter was visiting him. One evening she went out with friends. On her way back, driving alone at one in the morning, she hit a man. The man's body went flying across the road. The girl pushed down on the gas pedal and fled. When she arrived home, she told her father what she'd done and he, seeing how terrified she was, decided to shield her. He drove back over the road and found the body. For one awful minute, he thought it was breathing; he decided to leave it anyway. He drove home, took the daughter's car into town, and drove it into a tree in the priest's front yard to conceal its already broken headlight. At the end of this account, the narrator speaks with God:

> I do not feel the peace I once did: not with God, nor the earth, or anyone on it . . . [But now] in the mornings . . . I say to Him: I would do it again. For when she knocked on my door, then called me, she woke what had flowed dormant in my blood since her birth, so that what rose from the bed was not a stable owner or a Catholic . . . but the father of a girl.
>
> And He says: I am a father too . . .
>
> True . . . And if one of my sons had come to me that night, I would have phoned the police and told them to meet us with an ambulance at the top of the hill.
>
> Why? Do you love them less?
>
> I tell Him no, it is not that I love them less, but that I could bear the pain of watching and knowing my sons' pain, could bear it with pride as they took the whip and nails. But You never had a daughter and, if You had, You could not

have borne her passion.

So, He says, you love her more than you love Me.

I love her more than I love truth.

Then you love in weakness, He says.

As You love me, I say, and I go with an apple or carrot out to the barn.

"A Father's Story" moves forward under the influence of a disturbing piece of social, if not religious, orthodoxy—God is to man as man is to woman—akin to the sense of things that lies behind the Marine and loss-of-virginity stories. It posits, in Catholic terms, a hierarchy of existential vulnerabilities that mythicize men, women, love, and the mystery of life. It is hard to know what Dubus wants to say with such a conceit, especially now, when so many women and men are struggling to meet at eye level, to extend a hand across the open ditch that surrounds each of our lives. Who among us is to be moved or comforted by the assurance that we

170

are *all* as children commended to the care and pity of a Fatherly Being, but that, still, only a son need bear the consequences of his act?

Life is a Christian drama for Dubus's characters precisely because they understand so little about themselves in a world where self-understanding has become crucial. These people are bewildered; they act badly and are held accountable. Nevertheless, they are innocent. This, for Dubus, is religious metaphor: from it he derives his strength. Damnation mesmerizes him, holds his full attention, compels his deepest response. He may not have very much more understanding than his characters do of why their lives grow empty, but the emptiness itself he feels brilliantly: the look and the taste of it, the anguish it causes and the compromised inner peace to which it leads.

In Dubus's work, as in that of Carver and Ford, strength of feeling for the desolation in American life has brought new vitality to the kind of story that is famous for a hard surface beneath which spreads a contained flood of sentiment. But inside that tender toughness these stories have always seemed to be asking, "Why aren't things the way they used to be?" And, essentially, that's what they're still asking.

The despair of these writers can never be as moving to a reader like me as it is to the writers themselves. At the heart of their work lies a keen regret that things are no longer as they once were between men and women, a regret so intense that it amounts to longing. It's this longing, endowed with the appearance of hard reality, that informs much of their writing. But from where I stand, the hard reality is this: that question about why things are not as they once were has got to be asked honestly, not rhetorically. Then something more might be known about why life is so empty now, and the work of writers as good as Andre Dubus, Raymond Carver, and Richard Ford would be wise as well as strong.

James Baldwin and V.S. Naipaul: America Made the Difference

TWO MEN OF COLOR: ONE BLACK, ONE brown; one American, one Trinidad-Indian; both in a bottomless rage over having been born outsiders into a world dominated by whites; both released into a genius for writing by the force and influence of that very rage. If ever there were a pair of writers who, with roughly equivalent results, made the same virtue out of the same enduring necessity, surely it was V.S. Naipaul and James Baldwin. But it is the difference, not the sameness, between them that is compelling.

Born in Trinidad in 1932 into a large, noisy Indian family whose grandfathers had come to the island as indentured servants, Naipaul wanted out from childhood on. Everything about Trinidad and Indian family life made his skin crawl. At eighteen, he won an Oxford scholarship and went off to England, never again to live on the island. In England—now a man without a country—he suffered an unspeakable panic, and a loneliness that sent him into a near clinical depression. But he came out of it, got his degree, went down to London, got a job at the BBC, and within five years began writing the Trinidad novels that readers of English everywhere quickly recognized as the work of a strong literary talent. Then, at thirty-two, he went to India to discover the country of his "roots." What he saw shocked and repelled him. Out of the repulsion he wrote an exciting and vituperous book called *An Area of Darkness*.

For the next twenty-five years Naipaul would repeat this experience. He traveled the

Third World (India, Africa, the Caribbean, and the Arab East), writing extraordinary journalism out of the sparking anger that had been put on hold during the breakdown years in England, turning some of it into even more striking fiction: the piece about Michael X and Black Power in Trinidad became *Guerillas*, the one about Moboutu Sese Seko and the Congo *A Bend in The River*. He had found his subject. Now, he had only to teach himself how to serve it. Which he did mainly by approaching journalism as though it were literary narrative.

Very few writers as gifted as Naipaul have given themselves so fully to nonfiction writing. He brings to the genre an extraordinary capacity for making art out of lucid thought, the human application he prizes above all else. Observe hard, think even harder, figure out what you are thinking in the simplest, clearest language, and you will arrive at narrative: that is his credo. Naipaul is a writer for whom language is the enemy (he despises beautiful writing as much as he does mysticism), and narrative has little or nothing to do with plot or character. So he looks hard, thinks even harder, then, of course, darts to an unexpected place in the psyche where a flash of intuitive insight allows him to make narrative, very often, the way the poet does rather than the essayist. Among hundreds of instances, here's one perfect illustration:

In a piece on India, Naipaul is telling us that the religious rites of Hinduism belong to the ancient world, that the holy cow is absurd, as are the caste marks and the turbans. Then he writes, "[They speak] of a people grown barbarous, indifferent and self-wounding, who, out of a shallow perception of the world, have no sense of tragedy." No sense of tragedy. Auden could have written that. Suddenly, in a single phrase, the reader is gripped by the meaning of cultural arrest, the way it can narcotize a people, drain off urgency, allow history to simply drift on.

It was in India that Naipaul realized that he didn't fit in anywhere: never had, never would. It had been an illusion to think he could make himself into an émigré English novelist. His mind, he realized, was his only home. He must occupy it. To go on looking hard at the kind of place he had come from—to see things *as they are,* in the here and now, without blinders or sentiment—was the rock on which he would build his church.

Refusing to put a good face on things became Naipaul's article of faith. The countries where everything and everyone within living memory had been subjected to empire, where no one had ever belonged, especially not the natives, these were countries, he came to believe, that were overwhelmed by the task of making modern society, and thus hopelessly disposed to lassitude, terror, and an overriding self-deception. Everywhere he went, he experienced—and didn't hesitate to say he experienced—intellectual deficiency and moral blindness masquerading as an assertion of "authenticity." He despised the Africanization of Africa in the 1960s and '70s, as well as Black Power in the Caribbean, the super spirituality of India, and the ever-present social illness of political Islam. He thought it all the mark of a fatal self-division within cultures that had vast need of a compensating single-mindedness if they were to go forward. He was, he felt, watching "people who are really ill-equipped for the twentieth century, light years away from making the tools they've grown to like." And for this he had no pity.

In a 1981 interview, Naipaul, speaking of the breakdown he had suffered thirty years before, revealed that, at the time, he had seen a doctor who recommended treatment. Everything the doctor had said Naipaul had recognized as true, and he had hated him for saying it and stopped seeing him. He had cured himself, he told the interviewer. It had taken two years, but he'd done it. "Intellect and will," he said, "intellect and will." This is exactly what he expects of the Third World: that it will "cure" itself, not through some long, harrowing search for self-understanding, but by an act of will that simply pushes back the hysteria of magic and myth, employing the kind of disciplined mental work it takes to create a society ruled by reason and historical analysis.

Writing about Argentina in the 1990s, a country to which Naipaul returned four times in twenty years, he observes:

> Politics reflect a society and a land. Argentina is a land of plunder . . . and its politics can be nothing but the politics of plunder . . . [It remains] an artificial, fragmented, colonial society, made deficient and bogus by its myths . . . The failure of Argentina, so rich, so underpopulated, twenty-three million people in a million square miles, is one of the mysteries of our time.

He sees the country itself as a piece of social arrest that can be traced to its beginnings. To the original Spanish invaders, South America meant "nothing but conquest." For Naipaul, the culture has never developed beyond this primitive hunger for loot. In Argentina, he says, the value of work done honestly, both for its own sake and for the sake of the common good, is "the missing moral idea."

A preoccupation with the missing idea dominates "Argentina and the Ghost of Eva Peron," providing the piece with both its organizing power and its exciting simplicity. There is only one problem with it. Not among all the scenes visited, or the history related, or the people evoked (including Borges), do we feel ourselves in the presence of a fully recognizable human being. Not a single Argentine sees what Naipaul sees. No one in the country suffers or laughs or hungers or regrets as we do. Nowhere do we experience the wit of local idiom, the eloquence of melancholia, the sorrow of sexual passion, or the devastation of intellectual impotence. In short, there is nothing in this piece to remind the reader that human beings and the worlds they make and occupy are richly mixed—even though it is always the mixture that makes us feel the life within ourselves when we read.

Naipaul is famous for casting this cold eye on a huge cut of the world. Actually, the coldness is overrated; there is warmth beneath it—the dangerous warmth of emotional identification. More often than not, we are in the presence of a writer aroused by the sight of people who look just like himself struggling to make themselves human—and failing, failing, failing. From this perspective his intelligence cannot be diverted.

Because his intelligence is his genius, to watch Naipaul think about what he is looking at in exactly the way that he looks and thinks, is to learn something of the mystery of art. The reader feels sharply, and all at once, how hard are the edges of an imagination operating within the limits of a determinedly absent empathy, how remarkable it is that the sentences produced by that hard-edged take achieve the magic of poetic insight.

To read Naipaul steadily is to experience something of the dilemma of an attraction that does not generate love. Three or four hundred pages of strong and original writing applied to a social critique that uniformly withholds sympathy leaves the reader both stimulated and unsatisfied. Inevitably, as the years pass, the experience grows less exciting: the lack of tenderness wears on the nerves.

JAMES BALDWIN—THE FRATERNAL TWIN of Naipaul—stood the burning question of race dynamics on its head by coming at it from the inside out. In a flash of existential insight, strong, true, and lasting, Baldwin saw that white hatred of blacks originates in a toxic fear of the self that, in turn, induces self-hatred in blacks; this self-hatred, he intuited, was stealing the lives not only of black people but of white people as well. The insight came early to him—in his twenties—and it provided him with an internal balance that organized his literary genius for a good fifteen years. Later on, as the liberationist movements of the 1960s and '70s gathered identity-politics steam, we could all see that women and men, gays and straights were also bound together in a formal aggression ruled by the same terrible dynamic; but it was Baldwin who, between the late '40s and the early '60s, laid it out in a series of essays remarkable then, remarkable now. One reads the early Baldwin today and thinks, this is like Keats: the wholeness of vision here, in this painfully mature youth, is astonishing.

With hindsight, it was a moment in contemporary black history—somewhere between Richard Wright and the Panthers—that Baldwin seems destined to have occupied. There he was in Paris in 1948, twenty-four years old, directly out of Harlem, and he did the thing that a born artist does: caught a zeitgeist and applied it to himself. All over the western world, war-weary intellectuals were documenting the existence of the alienated self. Baldwin, sitting in the cafes scorning smashed-up Europe as an irrelevancy, nevertheless quickened to its deeper urgencies. The "otherness" of one's *own* life began to work in him. His inner attention became drawn to the idea of "what one's imagination makes of other people," and he saw that the phenomenon cut two ways.

"It is one of the ironies of black-white relations," he wrote at this time, "that, by means of what the white man imagines the black man to be, the black man is enabled to know what the white man is." This was an "otherness" that made sense. The white imagining the black, who then reactively imagines himself, began to calm the anger perpetually threatening to overwhelm him. Once made conscious, these connections penetrated his defensiveness and released his mind to become, in his thoughts, both the black *and* the white American.

It was the writer in him that welcomed the complicated point of view. Under its influence, he was able to describe his situation with passion and with distance: the passion made him eloquent, the distance empathetic. When he discovered "the weight of white people in the world," he wrote, it was as though he had contracted a chronic illness whose characteristic symptom is an ever-returning rage:

> Once this disease is contracted, one can never be really carefree again, for the fever, without an instant's warning, can recur at any moment. It can wreck more important things than race relations. There is not a Negro alive who does not have this rage in his blood—one has the choice, merely, of living with it consciously or surrendering to it.

At the same time, he was also able to write:

> Any real change implies the break-up of the world as one has always known it, the loss

of all that gave one an identity, the end of safety. And at such a moment . . . one clings to what one knew, or thought one knew . . . Yet, it is only when a man is able, without bitterness or self-pity, to surrender a dream he has long cherished or a privilege long possessed that he is set free . . . All men have gone through this, go through it, each according to his degree, through their lives. It is one of the irreducible facts of life. And remembering this, especially since I am a Negro, affords me my only means of understanding what is happening in the minds of white Southerners today.

This ingenious travel back and forth between "us" and "them"—employed repeatedly in a single piece, sometimes even in a single paragraph—became woven into Baldwin's sentence structure. Inside its elastic tension he found he could be everything he wanted to be (rational, humane, and cutthroat all at the same time) in order to be what he really needed to be: a man diving down into himself to locate the source of the wound. The combination of emotional fury coupled with high-minded thoughtfulness and psychological insight acted like a magnet on his first readers in '50s America. It drew them close, closer, closer still, until they were inside his skin with him. Once he had them there, his words took fire and left those readers marked for life.

But Baldwin was standing between a rock and a hard place. In Paris he was meeting black Africans—men like himself of talent, education, and ambition—with whom he felt no kinship. Speaking in the third person, he wrote of how this surprising development repeatedly threw him up against himself.

> Yet as he [the black American] wishes for a moment that he were home again, where at least the terrain is familiar, there begins to race within him, like the despised beat of the

tom-tom, echoes of a past which he has not yet been able to face. He begins to conjecture how much he has gained and lost during his long sojourn in the American republic. The African before him has endured privation, injustice, medieval cruelty; but the African has not yet endured the utter alienation of himself from his people and his past. His mother did not sing "Sometimes I Feel Like A Motherless Child," and he had not, all his life long, ached for acceptance in a culture which pronounced straight hair and white skin the only acceptable beauty.

How vast was the complication of identity, how deep the pit into which his own had thrown him. Everywhere Baldwin looked in those years, he was thrown back on the fact that he was this *American*, as well as *this* American. He had been in Paris a couple of years before it became clear to him that black and white Americans knew each other better than any European could ever know them. "When it did . . .

I suffered a species of breakdown." The more clearly he saw the particularities of his situation, the more clearly he saw how alone he was in France. In *Equal in Paris,* a famous essay about having been falsely arrested, he wrote: "I began to realize that I was in a country I knew nothing about, in the hands of a people I did not understand at all . . . None of my old weapons could serve me here. I did not know what they saw when they looked at me."

To know himself, he concluded, he must be where he is seen by an other whom *he* could imagine. It was in service to describing accurately what was happening between himself and that white American whom he had kept alive in his head for a decade and more that Baldwin had produced memorable work—that murderous, truth-speaking voice of his doing for the American essay what George Orwell's did for its English equivalent—but now, in the late '50s, because he could not see himself in a Frenchman's eyes, and because he had been too long gone from home, he began to lose his inner bearings.

As the distance between himself and his experience grew, that live sense of the "other" began to disappear from the page. When it did, the acuteness of the writing blurred, and Baldwin's uncommon use of language lost power. The remarkable voice started to ring false, the vibrant sentences now sounding insistent and overwritten. As his excellent biographer James Campbell observes of a disappointing novel of this time:

> For every passage of vivid realization there is a corresponding one of purple prose; for every precise image an inflated one; for every taut exchange of dialogue a conversation that is allowed to run on . . . Sometimes it is hard to see that the pen which crafted the sentences of "Notes of a Native Son," "Alas, Poor Richard," and "The Black Boy Looks at the White Boy"—a pen that gives the impression that its versatility is unlimited—is responsible for *Another Country*.

In 1961, in the introduction to *Nobody Knows My Name,* Baldwin wrote:

> In America the color of my skin had stood between myself and me; in Europe, that barrier was down. Nothing is more desirable than to be released from an affliction, but nothing is more frightening than to be divested of a crutch. It turned out that the question of who I was was not solved because I had removed myself from the social forces which menaced me—anyway, these forces had become interior, and I had dragged them across the ocean with me. The question of who I was had at last become a personal question, and the answer was to be found in me.

It is often said of Baldwin that he was undone by the '60s; that, feeling left behind by the incendiary activism of the civil rights movement, he deliberately gave up the rich amalgam of his own distinctive English to court favor with rhetoric spouting militants. It's an analysis I don't subscribe to. It seems to me that the crisis of the '60s dovetailed with a crisis of the spirit within Baldwin himself that would have occurred no matter what was happening in the world.

I think it not a tragedy that Baldwin's power deserted him, but a miracle that he sustained it for as long as he did. For fifteen extraordinary years he had pursued, through his blackness, "the question of who I was" with an energy generated by the kinetic force of youth. That energy did for Baldwin what it had done for Naipaul: convert the inertia of depression into the animation of anger. Inevitably, however, youth goes, the depression seeps back, and it takes a shocking amount of self-knowledge to, with consciousness and deliberation, from deeper down than one has ever been, haul up a working renewal of spirit. That, as D.H. Lawrence said, takes some diving.

IT IS THE RARE WRITER WHO ACCOMPLISHES a reinvention of the self once the writing exhausts its own first fine rapture; neither Baldwin nor Naipaul were able to manage it. For each, racism—in the world, in themselves— was the central experience. Out of its deadly fallout, both made art, and in both the genius for writing as well as the burn-out were equally mixed. One vital difference, however, sets them apart from one another, and will perhaps ultimately determine the degree to which their work will be valued generations from now. That difference is America.

For all the brutish failures inscribed in the broken promises of the republic, America encouraged, in the most despised of its citizens, an ardor for self-possession that served Baldwin well. For Naipaul, growing up colonized, it was precisely otherwise: empire and all that empire left behind sealed him off from himself in ways that were bound to prove impoverishing. Each writer wished, above all else, to "see things as they are." For Naipaul, this has meant relentlessly accusing humanity of being the sum of its disabilities; for Baldwin it meant turning inward in the hope of understanding the world by observing how he himself had been formed and deformed by those very same disabilities. Looking straight down to the bottom of his own wounded spirit, Baldwin was freed to write so penetratingly that his work, at its best, feels visionary: an evocation of world and self writ so large that it promises to deepen the self-understanding of the responsive reader anywhere, anytime. In the final analysis, that experience is what keeps literature alive long after the circumstance of its birth has ceased to matter.

BOSTON REVIEW BOOKS

Boston Review Books are accessible, short books that take ideas seriously. They are animated by hope, committed to equality, and convinced that the imagination eludes political categories. The editors aim to establish a public space in which people can loosen the hold of conventional preconceptions and start to reason together across the lines others are so busily drawing.